Real Ghosthunters

True Supernatural Encounters

Patrick Olson,
Dave Christensen
&
Leslie Christensen

PublishAmerica
Baltimore

First printing

ISBN: 1-4137-1452-8
PUBLISHED BY PUBLISHAMERICA, LLLP
www.publishamerica.com
Baltimore

Printed in the United States of America

Introduction

This book is a compilation of several actual cases that the Paranormal Investigations team has worked over the last several years. They have worked on hundreds of cases all across the United States. Their reputation has spread outside the boundaries of the United States and they have actually received calls from overseas requesting help with paranormal problems.

You can contact Dave and Leslie Christensen through their website, www.paranoramal-investigations.com.

Dave and Leslie Christensen founded the company in 1995 and took on some additional team members during their initial investigation. Kel and Darby came on board originally as skeptics. After their first case working with Dave and Leslie at Ball Cemetery, they quickly changed their minds and became firm believers in the paranormal.

Later on, another husband and wife team joined the team. Their names have been changed to protect their identities and they are called Randy and Kelly in the book. Randy suddenly died after being plagued by demonic nightmares for several weeks. The nightmares were related to the case and entity in the first chapter, The Devil in Worcester. Randy had told his wife that the entity in his dreams was going to kill him. His wife, Kelly, has not worked with Paranormal Investigations since the death of her husband in November of 2001.

As a child, Dave Christensen could *see* ghosts, literally. He actually had the ability to see them but as he grew older that ability gradually faded away. Then, when Dave was about 21, he lost his father. Soon after losing his father, his grandparents passed away. Before he knew it, half of his family was gone.

He was devastated and wondered if there was a tomorrow. Would he ever see them again? As a Catholic, his beliefs told him that yes, there is an afterlife. Being the curious person Dave is, he wanted proof, *concrete proof* that there is life after death.

In May of 1995, his first wife Debbie passed away from a heart attack. She was a very petite woman, 5'7", 115lbs and showed no signs of any health or heart problems. She suddenly died one night of a massive heart attack, leaving Dave to care for their four children. He decided right then that he *had* to know about the other side. Is there life after death?

He started by searching the Internet, scouring any sites related to ghosts. He found numerous sites that had information about ghosts, telling about what they can and can't do. He saw the pictures and the stories that they had on the sites but this *still* wasn't enough proof for Dave, *he had to see for himself.* He had to find and see ghosts with his own eyes to be certain of their existence. This would be the only way to prove to Dave that there is really life after death.

Dave met Leslie after he had been doing his research for a while but he didn't want to tell her right away about his interest in the paranormal. After they got to know each other better, Dave decided he would take her someplace. The first place he wanted to show her was Ball Cemetery in central Nebraska. He had been dating her for a few months and went to pick her up one day and he asked her " if he could take her some place unusual." Not exactly sure what he meant by "unusual," she was reluctant but finally agreed to go.

Leslie picked up the account here and recounted that they arrived at Ball Cemetery after dark and it was a very bright moon that night. The cemetery was "one of the spookiest places I've ever been and it looked like one of those places in a 60's werewolf movie." The cemetery was lined with tall trees and the moon shimmering off of the headstones made plenty of creepy shadows. It gave her the creeps, but they walked around to check it out as Dave took some pictures. Then they walked outside the cemetery for a while and they were standing at the fence when, suddenly, Leslie was kicked in the shin by some unseen entity. She didn't see anything at the time but certainly felt the kick and had a large bruise the next day to prove it. Odd.

Eager to see if anything unusual turned up on the pictures, they excitedly dropped them off at the 1-hour photo at K-Mart the following day. When they returned and picked up the finished pictures they were very surprised at what they were looking at. They had some incredible photos with ghostly apparitions that they couldn't explain. In addition, Leslie had a huge bruise on her shin to bolster her own belief. She had been standing still, so how did the bruise get there? They were intrigued and hooked on ghost hunting at that point. They made it their lifelong career from that moment on, to continue to search for the paranormal and they delved into this headfirst. They married on August 13, 1999 (Friday the 13th) and have continued to research this topic from every angle together. They regularly consult with experts across the county in parapsychology, physics, mathematics and even chemistry in order to learn more and gain any insight on the paranormal.

They always have outside witness's work the cases with them in order to provide more legitimacy to their work. These have included police personnel, physicists, TV reporters, college professors, homeowners and their relatives to name a few. Dave and Leslie have sworn affidavits from several of these witnesses to attest that the events they have stated actually happened, just like they have recounted.

I happened across the Christensens by accident, much like the woman from the Prague case (see The Prague Connection chapter), who stumbled across their web site while searching for a completely different web site. I had been researching a reportedly haunted house in Iowa when I came across a link to Paranormal Investigation's web site. I don't really know why at the time, but I wrote down their name and phone number and put it in a desk drawer, forgetting about it until several months later.

I remembered the name and phone number I had written down several months earlier after some very odd things began to happen at my house in the Fall of 2002. I called Dave and Leslie for some advice and I found that they were very kind, helpful and knowledgeable. They certainly seemed to know their paranormal stuff and I was convinced that they were the real deal after taking their advice and getting some incredible video of orbs in my home.

There is no doubt in my mind that good and evil forces are all around us, watching and waiting. I believe that there are ghosts who are stuck in between earth and heaven or hell for reasons unknown to us. These are the souls of departed humans who roam the earth and take up residence with the living. I *know* they're here. Dave and Leslie *know* they're here. They've seen them, felt them, heard them, smelled them *and have been thrown across the room by them!*

Dave and Leslie's mission is to research the paranormal activity in a scientific manner in order to gather proof that it actually exists. They also help people in need along the way by investigating the paranormal activity in their homes and, in some cases, convince the entity or entities to leave the scared families' homes or at least leave them alone. They aren't on a crusade to convince people that ghosts exist, they *know* they do. People either believe in ghosts or they don't, and either way is fine with them because *they* know the truth.

For every answer they get, they have five more questions that come up, so there's no doubt that this will be an ongoing quest.

Here are their encounters with the supernatural.

Chapter 1

The Devil in Worcester

May, 1997. The phone rang at the busy Omaha, Nebraska hospital in the middle of the day shift. "Leslie, it's for you," a voice called out. The phone was handed to Leslie Christensen on this otherwise uneventful day at the hospital. "Leslie, this is Kelly Roe! We're at Randy's cousin's house in Massachusetts and things are going on, I don't know what to do! Randy's possessed by something! His blood pressure is way up and his heart rate is really high!" Kelly was hysterical and very concerned for Randy, her husband, who had become possessed by something while they were on vacation and staying with Randy's cousin in Worcester, Massachusetts. Leslie responded, "Kelly, listen to me, keep an eye on Randy's blood pressure and don't leave him alone!"

Kelly called three more times during their "vacation" in Worcester to speak with Leslie. Leslie and Kelly both work at an Omaha, Nebraska hospital and certainly know how to deal with medical situations. Randy's medical situation had no logical answers. His symptoms were very high blood pressure, high heart rate, nausea, pale complexion and no appetite to mention a few. Some of his other symptoms included speaking in Latin, which he didn't know, and then suddenly snapping out of whatever was gripping him and having no recollection of the previous 40-60 minutes. After he would "snap out of it" he would be physically and mentally exhausted. During this first "vacation" encounter, Randy lost 30 pounds in two days. They wrapped up the visit and returned to Nebraska and it took Randy about a full month before he started feeling better and more like his normal self.

Randy desperately wanted to get back to Worcester to help his cousin Jesse and her 16 year-old daughter Kim. The reason they went there on "vacation" to begin with was because Jesse and Kim were being terrorized by some unknown entity. Over the previous few weeks Jesse had been beaten, held down in her own bed, unable to move, and nearly suffocated by some unseen entity in her own home. On several occasions household objects would suddenly fly through the house and at either Jesse or Kim and both were horrified. It came to the point where they would both come home and take a shower, change and leave as they were both too afraid to stay there, let alone sleep there another night. They were afraid of what awful things might happen next.

Kelly and Randy both wanted Leslie and her husband Dave to come out to Worcester to work the case and help Randy's cousin, who was desperate for help, any help! Dave and Leslie are very modest, hard working people who have a nice farm and home but don't have a lot of excess money. They generously help people with their supernatural problems and ask only that the people requesting their services pay for their traveling expenses (gas or plane fare), lodging and meals. They graciously take the time to travel all over the country to investigate supernatural occurrences and help whenever they can. Leslie said that she feels they are doing "Gods will" by helping people who are terrorized by the supernatural. They are both very sincere, down-to-earth people and are the kind of people who would help out a stranger with a flat tire on a dark, rainy night. They quickly agreed to help but needed to first save up some money for the trip to Massachusetts.

September, 1997. Other unusual events were going on in Worcester. Dave and Leslie were preparing to go there to help Randy's cousin. Unfortunately, they didn't have all of the money saved that they needed in order to make the trip. In September of 1997, a very unusual lightning storm developed and hung over downtown Worcester for two hours. The very unusual storm made national news because it was one large cloud that sat over Worcester, giving them one spectacular light show! There was no storm front, however, just the large cloud.

The following week on the TV show "Unsolved Mysteries," there was a story about a young girl who was hit by a bus and was in a coma. The child

8

remained in a coma and her parents decided to move her home for long-term care. A statue at the local Catholic Church started seeping an oily substance from her eyes, like she was crying. The church declared it a miracle and believed it was in some way tied to the girl who was still in a coma. The oily substance was believed to heal the sick, except it didn't heal the girl who remained in a coma. The church does believe that the girl in a coma is the cause of the healing oil.

It occurred to the Christensens that there seemed to be a battle between good and evil taking place in Worcester. At the very least there were certainly some very odd events happening, events that made national news at the time.

November, 1997. Dave and Leslie finally had picked a time to go to Worcester to help Randy's cousin. They finally had the money saved up to go. Suddenly, an unforeseen financial problem crept up and they were forced to use the money that was earmarked for the trip to Worcester. Back to square one, or so they thought.

A few days later a man showed up at the hospital in Omaha where Leslie works and was asking for her. She didn't recognize him and was sure she had never met this man before but approached him to see what he needed. As Leslie approached the man he said, "You need to go to Worcester, here's something for you." He quickly handed Leslie an envelope and walked down a hallway, turned the corner and was quickly out of sight. Leslie was amazed that this stranger would mention Worcester and she was curious to see what was in the envelope. She quickly opened it and was shocked to find five brand new hundred dollar bills, enough money for plane fare to Worcester. However, Leslie didn't want to accept the money from this kind stranger and quickly ran after him, turning the same corner he did moments before but he was gone. Thinking that maybe, for some odd reason, this stranger had ducked into one of the offices, she checked the doors in the hallway but they were all locked. There was nowhere this man could have gone so quickly because the doors were all locked in that hallway but he was gone! Leslie was determined to find this man and give him back his money. She put the envelope in her purse so that if she happened to see this man again she could give him back his money. The stranger was not seen again so Leslie could not return the envelope he had given her and the trip was back on to Worcester. The trip was back on and about to happen when, suddenly, Dave's mother became gravely sick and was quickly admitted to the hospital with a large tumor that had suddenly developed.

The doctors decided to operate and when they had Dave's mother opened up on the operating table they discovered cancer in the lymph nodes, kidneys and liver. Somehow they had not detected the cancer prior to the operation and the doctors could do nothing at this point because the cancer was too advanced so they stitched her up. Dave didn't want to leave for Worcester with his mother so gravely ill but she insisted that they go.

While at the hospital, Dave, Leslie, Randy and Kelly proceeded to the cafeteria for a little lunch after seeing Dave's mother, knowing her prognosis wasn't good. Once in the cafeteria, an old man approached Kelly and said, "Something weird is going on in Worcester, Massachusetts. If you want to know more, I'll be in ER." Kelly had never seen this man before and was floored by this unusual encounter and the fact that he mentioned Worcester. She also wanted to know more and went to find this man in ER but she never found him. She has not seen this man since that odd encounter in the cafeteria. This second stranger that suddenly appeared was not the same man that had approached Leslie prior to this. Dave and Leslie were also surprised to see that Worcester kept coming up. Why were strangers suddenly appearing with money, and strangers even mentioning the word Worcester? Most people have never even heard of Worcester and think that's a sauce that you put on your steak! It seemed to the group that something was driving them toward another "vacation" in Massachusetts. This something made Leslie very uneasy.

What forces were at work here? There certainly appeared to be some forces at work, both good and maybe not so good, driving the group toward an encounter with the entity that plagued Jesse and Kim. There seemed to be some positive forces at work, helping the group overcome their obstacles so they could make the trip to Worcester but at the same time it seemed like some darker, more sinister forces were at work trying to stop the trip altogether by throwing up roadblocks.

After the many hurdles, the time had finally arrived to fly out to Worcester and the group was ready. The flight route was from Omaha to Chicago and from Chicago to Boston. They were going to drive from Boston to Worcester. Dave and Leslie set out for the Omaha airport, hoping for an uneventful flight to Massachusetts. They had planned to reach Worcester in the early afternoon and set up their equipment, including motion detectors, sound equipment and video cameras. They had also hoped to get some rest before the "vacation" really started. As they pulled up to the long-term parking ticket booth they encountered a slight problem. It appeared that the ticket machine had just run out of tickets and they could not enter the parking lot. A lot attendant soon appeared and checked the machine and, sure enough, it was out of tickets. She said she'd be right back after she retrieved more tickets. She proceeded to her office but quickly realized that now there was another problem; she had just locked herself out of the office and her keys were inside. She had to contact Security to unlock the office and retrieve the tickets and this took some valuable time, time that Dave and Leslie didn't have as their flight was about ready to leave! They rushed into the airport, through security and they just barely made it to the gate with seconds to spare. The gate personnel were holding the plane for them because the ticket agents had notified the gate personnel of the situation. The ground crew quickly loaded their luggage and prepared the plane for takeoff. Dave and Leslie were just excited that they caught the flight after encountering all of the problems. Now they could finally sit back and relax for a little while because they would be in Massachusetts shortly.

They finally were off the ground and relieved that nothing else had gone wrong. They were on to Chicago at last. After landing in Chicago for what was supposed to be a forty-five minute layover, they were told that it would be a while before they could leave again. It seems that President Clinton was in town and Air Force One was at the airport and they were not letting any air traffic move while the President was nearby. Wasn't that just great? The forty-five minute layover stretched into a five-hour ordeal, further pushing back the much-awaited trip. Their flight managed to leave Chicago and arrived in Boston much later than they had hoped for. Now they still had the drive to Worcester looming ahead of them.

Day 1 in Worcester

They pulled into Worcester and arrived at Jesse and Kim's house about ten p.m., not getting the much-needed rest nor dinner before setting up shop.

It was now dark out and they were tired from a long day of traveling through busy airports. Business called though, and they were determined to get to the bottom of the activity in the house. The first thing they did was to walk through the house to "get a feel" for it and see if they had any uneasy feelings. They had spoken with Jesse and gotten her opinion on the house, now it was time to see what they could come up with. Dave slowly walked through the old house, trying to see if it would give up any of it's secrets, going from room to room. Up on the second floor there was an addition to the house, a back porch area that really made Dave feel uneasy. Something just didn't feel right about that part of the house. After going through the whole house he decided to set up the motion detectors first, that way if anything "came into the area" as Dave says, they would know about it. He set up the first motion detector facing a long hallway that lead to the creepy second story porch area because he felt very uneasy about this area. The second he turned away from the motion detector, it suddenly went off! Someone, or something, was coming down the hallway from the spooky room at the back of the house! It immediately "went into" Randy, who let out an unearthly, spooky roar like you have never heard before. Randy had been standing in the room and suddenly he was acting very strangely.

Randy's personality immediately changed. He started pacing the room, then started ranting and raving, occasionally stopping with a very strange stance, not at all like the Randy everyone in the room knew. Randy, Kelly, Leslie and Dave were all present in the room when this started to unroll, like a Steven King horror story, but this was real, and it was happening right in front of their eyes! Everything had immediately changed in the room and now even Randy's voice was different. He started ranting in a very strange voice, "The game is on, the game is on!" He then proceeded to speak in Latin, which he didn't know. Dave and Leslie began to follow Randy around with the audio equipment and were asking him questions but he would not respond. He continued to blurt out phrases in Latin, occasionally uttering other phrases in English like, "It's a battle zone!" and "Now it's gonna start and you're going to lose!"

Dave and Leslie watched as this scene unfolded in front of them. They noted the physical changes in Randy but also noted that he still had his Massachusetts accent. Initially, Dave thought that Randy was just putting on an act. On the other hand, the whole moment seemed surreal! Leslie found it hard to believe that Randy would spend so much money and have the Christensens spend so much money and time to fly out there to the east coast just to pull their chain with a prank. It just wasn't like Randy to do that.

They were all concerned about this development but, being professionals, they pressed on with the investigative work. They set up the rest of their equipment including three camcorders placed in strategic parts of the house and turned them on. Just as soon as they would turn on all of the camcorders, they discovered that the entity would go right behind them and turn them back off. They soon discovered that it would be a battle just to keep the equipment on and recording. After this hectic and frightening first few hours, they stopped about two a.m. and headed over to a neighbor's house for a short three-hour rest to recharge their exhausted bodies.

Day 2 in Worcester

Prior to going into the house in Worcester, Dave and Leslie had researched the property and history of the house for any clues to the unnatural activity that was occurring there now. They had found in the course of their research that a little boy had disappeared in 1932 and was never found.

During the first twenty-four hours of possession, Randy recounted a story of the death of Kevin, a little boy who had lived in the house in the 1930's. During the eerie account of Kevin, the year 1932 was mentioned. Randy, who was possessed at the time, went on in further detail. He stated that Kevin's father was a small, quiet man who was emotionally abused by his wife. The wife was a large, angry, pushy woman. As time went by, the mousy little husband started to crack under the relentless abuse from his wife. His wife made him sleep in his own room and as time went on, he started sexually abusing his six year-old son. During one of his assaults the father suffocated the boy and he died. During this part of the story, Randy started saying, "Your mother made me do this! It is her fault!"

Day two began about five a.m. and turned into a very long day of constant confrontation, one right after another, between Randy, who was still possessed, and Dave. Randy would constantly get into his friend's face and antagonize him and make threats, trying to goad him into a fight. Dave was well aware of what the entity was trying to do. He knew that Randy was not himself, literally, and knew that in order to defeat this entity, he had to remain calm and not show any anger or fear towards it.

Leslie started day two feeling very apprehensive. She had a very bad feeling about what they were going to encounter. Several weeks before leaving for Worcester, Leslie began having dreams about what was going to happen. She knew from her dreams that the entity was very malevolent, very evil. To add to her fears she was well aware of all the things that this entity had done to Jesse and Kim. Then, about three weeks before leaving for Worcester, Leslie had a dream about her dad, who comforted her and told her that she "didn't have to worry, everything was going to be alright. Nothing evil will touch you." Her dad had been dead for four years and the dream seemed to comfort her in this evil setting. Her dad reassured her that she would be OK and this gave her strength and determination to continue to battle this entity. After the first night's events and seeing what day two had brought, there was no doubt in anyone's mind who was witness to this unfolding scene that what they were up against was pure evil, a demonic entity. They were battling the devil himself and it was a race to save not only Jesse and Kim but now Randy as well. The devil had taken over his body, at least for now.

Randy continued to be possessed by the evil entity, confronted Dave all day long shouting threats, using foul language and occasionally speaking in Latin. He would be possessed for about twenty to forty minutes at a time. He then would snap out of it and act more like himself for thirty to forty-five minutes before the entity would regain control over him. When he was actually himself, he would have no recollection of the events that occurred while he was possessed. He was physically and mentally exhausted and felt very sick.

Leslie had also recalled that she had in her pocket an item that her son gave her before they left for the Omaha airport. He told her, "This is my strength, take it with you." He had given her a small item wrapped in a rag that she had immediately put in her pocket and kept in her pocket throughout the entire stay. He was concerned for her safety. Leslie never looked to see what her son had wrapped up in the rag. The fact that her son gave it to her and was concerned for her was good enough and gave her some comfort. Only after they finished the case did she look to see what was in the rag. She found that her son had taken a small dragon off of his prized sword, along with a chunk of his hair that he had cut off. These two items had been carefully wrapped up in the rag to protect his mother and give her strength against the unknown forces that they were up against.

The confrontations were escalating and Randy was pushing Dave, trying to get his friend to hit him while saying awful things and using foul language. Things looked like they were just about ready to explode between Randy and Dave when Leslie walked in between the two men and put her hand on Randy's chest and said firmly and forcefully, "Stop!" Randy looked surprised and said, "Get your hand off me!" to which Leslie replied, "No!" Randy then asked, "Why are you doing this?" and Leslie replied, "Because I can!" The still-possessed Randy looked surprised and angry at the same time. He seemed paralyzed; he couldn't move from the spot he was standing on in the middle of the floor. Leslie was getting nervous at this point and was concerned that if the men became violent that they would lose control of the situation and the negative energy would feed the entity, allowing it to become stronger. Dave realized this and knew this going into this situation. He used every ounce of his self-control to remain calm and not show any anger or fear towards the entity/Randy. Dave seized the opportunity and calmly walked away from Randy, who was still standing in the middle of the room with Leslie's hand firmly planted on his chest.

It was an odd sight to see this man who was possessed ranting and raving, and spewing filthy language and insults towards Leslie. For whatever reason, he stood there and Leslie stood her ground with her hand still firmly on his chest. Why wasn't this demonic entity able to simply brush away Leslie's hand from his chest and continue the confrontation? Leslie then pulled her hand back and Randy took a few steps and staggered. He, or it, looked surprised at the turn of events. Exactly how powerful was this entity? Could it be defeated? Leslie, at that very moment, was sure that no evil would be able to touch her as she recalled the dream of her father who comforted her and told her that no evil would be able to touch her. Also, at that very moment, her strong conviction and faith in God gave her great comfort and confidence to stand up to this evil entity. She firmly believed that God would protect her from this most pure form of evil, standing a few steps away from her. So far, she was right.

Throughout the last two days, Randy, while possessed, was going around the entire house carving V's into everything, including the floors and walls. Dave and Leslie later found out that the V it was carving stands for Voorhea, which means demonic human.

Dinnertime ever so slowly arrived and the group managed to find time to make dinner. Even Jesse and Kim stopped by for this, although they were not overly excited about it. Randy was drifting in and out of being possessed throughout this whole ordeal and you never would know when it would leave him alone. When he was not possessed he was constantly drained of all energy and felt very sick. His blood pressure was sky high, his heart rate was dangerously high, his skin was pale, he was sweaty and he felt like he would vomit if he ate anything. Leslie, always watching out for Randy, said, "Randy, at least drink some water or milk or something!" but he wasn't in the mood for any food. Leslie and the rest of the team and even Jesse and Kim proceeded to eat dinner.

Without warning, the flames on the decorative little candles that were on the center of the table started to dance up and down two to three inches at a time. Leslie suspected she knew why and slowly looked over at Randy who was seated right next to her. He was grinning an ominous grin that unnerved her. Leslie then asked Randy, "What?" He continued to grin and stare. He replied in a voice that didn't quite seem normal, "Your soul is at stake." Leslie countered, "My soul has never been at stake. I am very assured of where I'm going after I die, are you?" With this the candles then started dancing five to six inches high. Leslie then asked Randy, "Are you doing this?" She was referring to the candle flames unnatural movements. Randy replied, "I have the power." Suddenly, the candle flames shot up to about a foot high from these little decorative candles! It seemed impossible but it was happening! After dancing unnaturally high, the flame dropped back down to the normal height after several tense moments. Randy, or the entity, was visibly angry that he couldn't get a reaction out of Leslie. Leslie told Randy, "That's just a parlor trick, anybody can do a parlor trick!" This seemed to be increasing the tension level and Randy, or the entity, certainly didn't like being mocked and brushed off as insignificant. Its anger was growing and very apparent.

Dave then jumped on the bandwagon and started to antagonize Randy too, to see if he could get a reaction out of the entity. Dave said, "You're just weak, I can do that too. You're nobody!" He threw in a few other choice words and this really pushed the entity's buttons. Randy/the entity immediately jumped up and started pacing the floor in the kitchen, ranting about how powerful he was. He then paced over to Leslie and leaned over the arm of her chair and whispered in her ear, "I'm gonna get your soul, I'm gonna get your soul." She calmly replied after slowly reaching down and taking bites of food, "No, no you're not. Get off it, you know darn well I'm secure." She casually reached down and took a drink of water. Randy then proceeded to walk around the table to Kim, Jesse and Kelly, doing the same thing to try and rattle them.

Dave then decided to pipe in and told Randy, "You can't pick on the women anymore, they've got your number and they're not afraid." The anger visibly grew inside the entity as everyone was sitting there laughing at him and he wasn't getting the reaction that he had hoped for from this tough crowd. Dave and Leslie had told Jesse and Kim before dinner, "Don't show him any fear, don't back down to him, laugh in his face and make light of it. You have to push him further and further away and he'll go, we'll drain him of his energy." The entity became enraged and started literally stomping through the kitchen and told Dave, "I'll show you, come to my domain and I'll show you!" Dave calmly replied, "Fine." Scooting back his chair, he stood up to follow Randy to "his domain." Dave followed Randy back to the creepy second floor porch room where he had initially felt some uneasiness. The room was in the shape of a half-moon and there was a stool in the center of it. As they walked into the room a strange thing happened. Randy's hair stood straight out and up, like it had a massive amount of static electricity in it. Nobody else's hair did this, just Randy's. His long hair and pony tail wildly stood straight out and looked like a wild afro from the '70's. Dave plopped down on the stool, showing no fear to the entity and said, "OK, I'm here, show me what you got, show me how big and bad you really are!" Randy, or the entity, stood in front of Dave who was seated about in the center of the half-moon room, and proceeded to bend his arms at the elbows upwards and cross them. He then let out a very loud roar, like a lion, and every window in the room literally exploded with a resounding boom! Everyone in the house quickly voted with their feet to exit the house and Dave heard only the noise of footsteps making a hasty retreat down the stairs and the sound of broken glass falling to the ground and floor below!

The women nervously called up from outside to the now broken out windows to Dave to see if he was OK. "Are you OK, are you OK up there?" He was OK, but freaked out and momentarily not sure what to do or say. This thing was powerful, standing right in front of him and very angry! Dave quickly gathered his thoughts in a split second and blurted out, "OK, I'm impressed, now can you levitate?" Randy went stomping out of the room in a rage. The women were still trying to see if Dave was OK and called up again, "Are you all right?" He leaned out one of the broken windows and replied, "Yeah, I'm OK, I really got him going now, he can't levitate!" Leslie shot up, "Are you crazy, get out of there!" She was very concerned for everyone's safety at this point. Instead of getting out of the house, Dave followed Randy into another room and confronted him. Dave forcefully stated, "You haven't shown me anything, come on and levitate! If you levitate in front of me I will believe you! If you levitate, that might get me excited, otherwise you're nothing!" Randy stomped off and proceeded to stomp through the entire house from room to room in a rage because he wasn't getting the reaction he wanted from Dave or the group. After stomping through the house he then went into the back bathroom and shut the door.

All of the women were really stressed at this point. They were scared and surprised at the power of this entity. They were also concerned for their safety after the powerful display the entity had just put on for them. Leslie was especially concerned because their other team members were Randy, who was presently possessed, and Kelly, who did not have any training to prepare her for this terrifying situation. This was really new to Kelly and this left Dave and Leslie to basically cover each other's backs and it could become very dangerous, so there was some genuine concern at how this situation was unfolding.

Randy was still in the bathroom so Dave and Leslie grabbed the tape recorders and hit the record button because they could hear talking in the bathroom. They didn't understand what he was saying but they proceeded to tape it anyway so they could listen to it later. They soon discovered that it was in Latin. The tape contained about twenty minutes of weird chanting and talking, although Randy was alone in the bathroom. They later took the tape to a Catholic Priest at Creighton University in Omaha, Nebraska to see if it could be translated. Part of it was translated and he was talking about the sacrificial lamb and King David and his war with the Canaanites. Not all of the tape was loud or clear enough for translation.

Day 3 in Worcester

The Christensen's had taken readings from all over the house in the course of the last two days and had gotten some good energy readings from the wall with a mirror on it in the room where the windows had blown out. The strange thing was there were absolutely no energy readings coming off of Randy the entire weekend although he clearly appeared to be possessed and they were all convinced of this, especially after the windows were blown out!

On the third evening in the house, Dave and Leslie decided to thoroughly search the house for any further clues to the strange activity that was occurring. While searching the attic they found an old dress, a size twenty-two. Then they found an old flight jacket, one that appeared to be WWI vintage. The flight jacket looked like it would fit a small man that was about 5' 5" and around 125 lbs. The jacket obviously was for a small man. This seemed to fit what Randy had recounted to a T. About ten o'clock that evening, Kim and Jesse brought the old clothing from the attic out into the yard and burned it, thinking it may have some connection to the horrifying events taking place in their home.

They all felt the negative energy leave the house on the third night at about 11:30- midnight, shortly after the clothing was burned in the yard. Dave and Leslie slept in the house that night and everything turned peaceful and calm. Even Jesse and Kim slept there, the first night in a long time that they actually stayed there. Dave and Leslie had to get up and head back to Omaha the next morning at five a.m. but they did manage to get some well-deserved sleep.

Dave and Leslie feel that they were able to defeat this demonic entity because they were able to use up it's energy. These entities feed off of negative energy created by fear, anger and hate and can be stopped by not giving it these emotions to feed off of. They relied on their vast experience and knew that they needed to remain calm and show no fear or anger towards the entity if they were going to have any chance to defeat it. They also relied on their faith in God and love for each other to deprive it of any negative energy. It finally saw that it wasn't going to beat them and left, for the time being anyway.

Jesse and Kim wasted no time moving from their house of terror but they moved only across the street. They were not plagued by the entity at their new house.

A couple moved into their former residence shortly after they moved out. The new couple fought all the time and within a year, the entity returned to the house. It was being fed by the negative energy the new couple were providing it.

Randy and Kelly returned to Nebraska and Randy was in very poor health for about a month after returning from the exhausting trip. He was sick all the time and everyone knew it was directly related to him being possessed in Worcester.

Was there a connection between the old clothing and the paranormal events in the house? Was a little boy murdered in this house long ago? If so, was the murder and negative energy somehow related to the recent problems that had been plaguing the current residents of the house? Time will tell.

Chapter 2

The Prague Connection

Prague, Nebraska is a small community in eastern Nebraska about a half-hour drive west of Omaha. The Midwest has a quality of life you can't beat. Quiet, spacious, laid-back and mostly rural. Many generations of families have grown up on the farm or in rural areas and enjoy the lifestyle. Some enjoy the location and not having neighbors too close, where others enjoy the beautiful land and seasonal changes. Some people are not so happy because they live in a haunted house. The last place you would expect a haunted house to be is out in the peaceful, Nebraska countryside, but that's exactly where this house was. Prague, Nebraska, small, peaceful and very haunted.

In the winter of 1999, Dave and Leslie received a call for help from a family out in the country near Prague, Nebraska. An older woman, her son and grandchildren moved into a dream home in the country. The dream home shortly turned into a living hell on earth. Within three months of moving into the beautiful dream home, things began to change for the worse. One of the grandchildren, she was two at the time, had a serious personality change immediately after moving into the new house. She changed from a loving little girl to a hellion. She quickly changed into a girl who was very obnoxious, violent and frequently slapped and hit people. She changed 100% in three months time. She was taken in for counseling and the doctors wanted to prescribe

This picture was taken from the doorway of the kitchen into the living room area, just shortly after someone said they heard a strange noise coming from the living room. After the picture was taken Randy, Leslie and Dave walked into the room. The temperature was noticeably cooler and there was a sensation of a draft in the room from time to time. Leslie said she could feel the presence of an elderly woman that lived there many years prior to that night. She felt that her children that lived there her entire life abused the woman. She also felt a younger woman, not related to the older woman, in the room. The younger woman felt confused about everything going on in the house.

medication but her problems ran deeper than that, much deeper. Medication couldn't help what was ailing her. The woman who rented the home became very depressed in a short three month span and she complained to Dave and Leslie that her son "saw shadows" in the house. She knew something was not right and she was very frightened. Her new dream house was turning into a nightmare!

Dave and Leslie, as usual, did their research on the property and house before launching the formal investigation. The research turned up some very interesting things about the property.

The last three original family members who owned the house all grew up and died on the property, along with their parents. None of them ever married or left the farm. Prior to their deaths, the kids had cared for their elderly mother and she never left the farm, literally. They never let her go into town or anywhere for that matter. People who knew her were told that the kids were physically abusive towards her, frequently hitting her. She lived there at the farmhouse until passing away in her 90's.

It turns out that the last three families that had lived in the old house had really bad things happen to them after moving in. Seven years prior to their investigation of the house, a family, family #1, moved into the house when it was up for rent. They were well liked, had two kids and were doing very well in the community. Within a year of moving in, the parents were arrested for child abuse and drug trafficking. When they were arrested if was found that they were locking their small children into a cellar under the house and going into town to run errands. They eventually were prosecuted, lost their kids and went to jail.

Family #2 moved in about three years prior to the investigation. A couple moved in that had a good relationship prior to moving into the house. Shortly after moving in, things began to change and the husband was charged with abuse for beating his wife. He had a good job but he lost it and they soon divorced.

Family #3 was the current family. Armed with their exhaustive research, Dave and Leslie assembled a team to investigate the house. The team included Kelly and Randy, a reporter, a Police Chief, a biologist and a professor from Creighton University in Omaha. They diligently made their way to the house. On the first night, Leslie went upstairs to a back room and suddenly experienced a total personality change. She is usually very energetic, enthusiastic person but suddenly felt very depressed and leaned against a wall with her back. The professor came up the stairs and, knowing Leslie and her normal personality, asked her, "What's wrong?" He noticed that she didn't look like her normal self. She replied, "Why do you think anything's wrong?" The professor responded, "You don't look like yourself, you don't act like yourself, what are you doing?" She replied without much enthusiasm, "I'm being very depressed and I don't want to be here. I'm going to go outside." She made her way downstairs because the upper rooms and atmosphere of the home were very depressing. Once downstairs she began to have very sharp pains in her stomach that continued for about fifteen to twenty minutes. The reporter then came into the living room on the first level of the house and stated that she was having some very sharp stomach cramps. Both the reporter and Leslie decided to go outside and sit in the car. It was really cold outside and neither one of them felt like standing outside in the cold. Within five minutes of leaving the house both Leslie and the reporter felt 100% better with no further stomach pains.

This picture was taken in the first bedroom at the top of the stairs. Randy told us that he could feel someone present in the room real close to him. He stated that he had children around him. In this picture you can see a number of orbs all around him in the room. There is one orb out in the hallway.

Randy was also being affected by something in this house. After two and a half years of being OK, something had taken a hold of him again. He began to get eerily similar symptoms to the case in Worcester. While standing in a back room of the house Randy began to talk about a family that used to live in the house. He began to go into great detail about a pregnant wife and a murder that occurred long ago. He also indicated the location of the body that he stated was buried on the property. The more they listened the more interesting it became.

He spewed out times, the exact date, names and even the weather conditions the night of the murder. While in some altered state, Randy stated that on the night of the murder of the pregnant wife on a long ago September night there was a torrential downpour. The date was September 19, 1938. A jealous husband killed his wife and wrapped the body up in a rug. He carried the body up a hill, falling once as he struggled with the slippery conditions, but he picked up the body in the rug and continued. He carried her past the big tree up the hill and dug a shallow grave. Next, he dropped the body in the shallow grave and covered it with rocks, then boards and then more rocks. Randy continued on with his unusual accounting of this long- ago murder and again stated that the body was buried past the large tree by the outbuilding.

Dave was again skeptical about Randy's account and thought maybe he was pulling a prank on them. Leslie, however, said she would reserve her opinion until after they had a chance to research the information they had just received, including the weather conditions for that particular day back in 1938.

Most of the details of what Randy blurted out were later verified through historical records, newspapers and Internet information. After two weeks of meticulous searching, they found the local newspaper archives for the date of the murder. There were torrential downpours on the night of the murder and it had rained for five days straight, just like Randy had stated. They also verified that a woman had been reported "missing" from that area at that time. The official records listed her as a runaway. The husband had stated that she had run off and it didn't appear that any formal investigation into her disappearance had taken place. Randy had said the husband murdered the wife because he believed that she was pregnant with someone else's child. Dave and Leslie found the "someone else" and he was very old but still alive. He was unaware of any murder, however.

All of the details that Randy stated had been verified except for the murder itself. The team used a probing rod to search around the site that Randy had described where the body was buried and within a few short minutes they located what they believe may have been the grave of the murdered wife. They encountered a problem at this point. Family #3 who was having problems with the house were just renting it and the property was still owned by relatives of the original family and they wanted no part of digging up graves. They certainly did not want any past misdeeds uncovered. If a grave were to be found that may prove another relative of theirs may have committed a murder 60+ years ago. This was something that they just didn't want to do. They refused to give the police permission to dig and so that aspect of the case remains a mystery, but the probing rod did hit a number of rocks precisely where Randy had described the grave. Rocks were described as being on the top layer of the grave and they were found about one to one and a half inches under the surface. This matched Randy's account of where the grave was and also how the grave was constructed.

This picture taken outside the house shows an incredible number of orbs in one location on the property. There are many entities haunting this house and property.

The entire time they worked this case Leslie was sick and depressed while at the property. Randy was always agitated and angry while at the house and would often throw things. He only gave information in an altered state on the first night at the property. The rest of the time he was just agitated and eventually Dave and Leslie stopped taking him there because he was starting to get sick again. This was starting to remind them of the Worcester case, the way Randy was acting. Nobody was really sure, but they didn't believe Randy had actually become possessed at this location but they also couldn't explain how he came up with this historically accurate information from 60+ years ago. He had not done any prior research on the property yet he knew precise details from the 1930's. Leslie believes that Randy was somehow open to whatever energy or entity was there and it was very detrimental to his health.

The entire time they were working this case Leslie was plagued with serious body pain and would frequently have to leave the house. After leaving the house the pain would dissipate. Around the third month of the investigation Leslie began to see some familiarity in this case but couldn't figure out the actual connection.

She felt that whatever was in the house was very familiar and very ancient. She stated that, "It's been around forever, it's older than people, older than the earth." Suddenly, it hit her like a ton of bricks and she turned to the professor and said, "I've got it!" He replied, "You know what it is now?" Leslie excitedly replied, "I've got it, it's just pure evil. It is the purity of evil in itself and I've felt this before." The professor, looking surprised, asked, "Where?" Leslie replied, "In Massachusetts. It's the same. I don't know how it manifests itself but it's the same energy and it knows me and it knows Dave." Dave agreed 100% in his assessment of the entity or energy that was in this Midwestern farmhouse. They didn't expect to encounter this same entity or energy again and were thrown off by the fact that the cases were very different. In Worcester the entity was physically attacking the occupants of the house and throwing things at them. In this case there was the drastic change in personality of the granddaughter along with some other odd things like the son seeing shadows in the house but that was about the extent of it. Dave and Leslie could feel the energy and knew something was there but didn't know exactly what it was until that defining moment when it became clear to Leslie.

However, there were some eerie similarities. The older woman had no idea Dave and Leslie even existed until one day when she was on the Internet and she had typed in a website completely different from theirs. Somehow, she was taken to their website and later gave them a call. It certainly seemed like she was somehow steered in their direction or was this just an odd coincidence?

After Leslie realized what they were up against, they were able to work the case much easier and they wrapped up the case shortly after that realization. They were able to get the ominous entity to leave but there are numerous other entities that still reside in the house and at the property there but they don't seem to bother anyone. The current residents have not reported any unusual activity there and hope to keep it that way. This case was completed in January of 2000.

Chapter 3

Death of a Friend

After returning from helping Dave and Leslie with the Prague, Nebraska case, Randy was again sick for about a month. He had been to the house on three occasions and on each occasion he would become very agitated, throw things and it seemed like his personality changed. After the third time going there and again acting this way, Dave and Leslie decided it was best if they didn't bring him along, for the sake of his own health which was suffering from the effects of whatever energy or entity was in the Prague house. Dave and Leslie had started that investigation in the winter of 1999 and concluded it in January of 2000.

Randy was also concerned about his health and the fact that whatever was in the homes in both Worcester and Prague could so easily invade him, literally. He was also concerned that the entity or entities may also be able to feed off his energy and grow stronger, making it more difficult for Dave and Leslie and the rest of the team to get rid of whatever was making the family in Prague so miserable.

About a month after he had stopped working with Dave and Leslie, Randy finally started feeling a little better and wanted to start working with them on cases along with his wife Kelly. Kelly had called Dave and Leslie to check into the possibility that they start working together again but she noted with some concern that Randy had been waking up in the middle of the night, screaming about terrifying nightmares with the entity that had possessed him in Worcester. Dave and Leslie were very concerned about this and Randy's health and told Kelly to call them back a little later and they would get together. In November of 2001, Leslie received a phone call from Kelly with some grim news. "Randy is dead," Kelly had stated. The emotion was very evident in her voice. "You're kidding?" Leslie asked, not knowing if Kelly was playing a prank on her. Kelly responded, "No, I'm not kidding you." Leslie was stunned, knowing Randy was only 42 years old. He wasn't overweight and his health had been better since he got away from the house in Prague, Nebraska. Leslie had to ask, "What happened?" Kelly answered, "I don't know. For the last three weeks he woke up every night screaming and he would have these nightmares about the entity in Massachusetts and it looked just like in the picture." In the dreams the entity was saying to Randy, "I'm waiting for you and I'm going to get you." And the entity was in the basement, waiting for Randy. Kelly then told Leslie that on Saturday morning, the day Randy died, he woke up at four in the morning and he was terrified. He was sweating and screaming and starting crying. He said, "We've got to call Dave and Leslie tonight, it's here, it's here, I know it's here! We've got to talk to them! We've got to stop this, it's going to kill me!" Kelly tried to calm Randy down and told him, "Hang in there, we'll call them when I get home from work." Kelly had to get to work at the hospital in Omaha. Randy then told Kelly that she needed to be prepared, that he was "going to die." His words rang very true.

Kelly proceeded to work, concerned about Randy but was hopeful they could do something about this terrifying situation after she returned from work later. After her shift, Kelly came home to find the back door still locked and Randy's car still in the driveway. She was puzzled at this because Randy was supposed to leave for work shortly after her and should have been at work. Kelly unlocked the door and was wondering why Randy didn't unlock the door for her because he usually did if he got home first. She slowly entered the house but didn't see Randy anywhere. She wasn't too concerned yet and thought that maybe he went to see one of the neighbors. Kelly then went into the bathroom and found Randy dead! She was horrified to find her husband dead but something was very eerie about this. He had gone into the bathroom and sat on the toilet and had put his arm on an armrest that was just below shoulder level. He sat there looking up at something on the ceiling. He was found in this same position, on the toilet sitting up straight, with an arm up on his homemade armrest, looking up at the ceiling with his eyes wide open! The question is, what was he looking at?

The autopsy showed the cause of death to be a heart attack. So, what caused this forty-two-year-old to die so young? What, if anything, did his dreams and nightmares have to do with his death? It has been said that the soul knows when it will be set free and it helps the mind to prepare for this. Were the nightmares just his own mind playing out his fear of dying? Or, did the evil entity that manifested his dreams literally frighten him to death? Another strange thing about this is that when people have a heart attack they don't usually die instantly. A sharp pain jabs the chest area and it can take several minutes before a person dies from this yet Randy was found sitting straight up on the toilet. You would think a person would be clutching their chest in pain and likely be on the floor, not sitting on the toilet after they passed away.

The Christensens don't know if they will ever be able to answer any of these perplexing questions, but they will continue to search.

Chapter 4

Dave's Dreams

Dave started having dreams about the demonic entity that they battled in Worcester. His dreams started in December 1997, a month after returning from Worcester. At the time, Dave was living in Omaha and was recovering from the harrowing ordeal a month earlier. It had been a physically exhausting case and he was drained of energy for several weeks.

Dave isn't sure why the dreams started or what they were supposed to mean. In his dreams he sees a large house out in the country in a beautiful setting. Leading up to the house is a very windy dirt road and it's lined with trees. For some reason, the house is only half built. The house is in a beautiful location and from the living room picture window you get a commanding view of the once wild plains of the Midwest. The house sits on a hill overlooking a river below about a mile away. Around the house it's fairly wooded and quiet. Except there are many ghosts in the house in his dreams. The house is very haunted with many spirits and the land around the house is also haunted. On the other side of the river are limestone bluffs that are dotted with caves and it's wooded in front of the limestone so you really can't see what's behind the trees until you're up close. The dreams turn more ominous as he is led or drawn to a dark cave on the other side of the river. It's hard to see the cave because the trees are there, you have to get closer, closer and the evil entity is waiting for him in the cave, wanting him to go inside but he doesn't, he knows better. He knows that this is it's domain. He can see it's eyes in the cave, it's waiting for him. Then he wakes up.

The dreams are always the same. The same haunted house, same windy road, same commanding view of the river and bluffs and yes, the same dark, ominous cave. The same demonic entity was waiting, waiting and watching.

The dreams started in December of 1997 after encountering the demonic entity in Worcester. The dreams continued off and on through mid 1999. After finishing work on the house in Prague, Nebraska the dreams continued for about another three months and then subsided. They started again in the summer of 2000 briefly and subsided again. More recently, he started having the dreams after we started collaborating on this book project in March 2003. The dreams have continued. He has the dreams two to three times per month and they're always the same. Here's where it gets really interesting.

Dave and Leslie wanted to move from the city life in Omaha and decided to buy a house in the country so they started looking within about a sixty-mile radius of Omaha. They found a beautiful house with seven acres of land and purchased this in September of 2000. The house is in a quiet, serene setting out in the country with a windy dirt road that's tree lined. The house had a half-finished edition on the side when they bought it, just like in Dave's dream. The house has a commanding view as it sits on top of a hill overlooking a river about a mile away. Across the river there are limestone bluffs, hidden behind the many trees and bushes and yes, there are caves that dot the limestone bluffs. The house is haunted with numerous ghosts; over thirty have been counted. They have pictures to prove it. They have seen at least three ghosts in their house in human form. They have seen a man, a woman dressed in late 1800's era clothes and a child. In the woods that surround the house in the back, they frequently see dancing orbs at night that dart in and out of the woods around the house. Leslie describes them as looking much like fireflies, "But you don't see fireflies in the wintertime." The orbs can be seen year-round. Many times the orbs will float towards their house and when they get close to the house they disappear. Then they will occasionally hear the basement door open and close, even when nobody is down there. They describe the orbs as glowing balls of light that vary in size, color and intensity. The orbs have been seen in white, green, blue and yellow and are anywhere from the size of a firefly to the size of a basketball. The intensity varies from nearly transparent to very bright, like a full moon on a clear winter night. They have numerous pictures of the orbs and ghosts that share their house and property.

Dave didn't realize that the house they purchased was the same house that was in his dreams until later when the dreams had started back up again. Then it suddenly dawned on him that this was the house in his dreams!

The mystery remains though, why was he drawn, or directed, to this house? What does this entity want with them or have in store for them? Why is it doing this? These questions may be answered soon. Dave is going to try and find the cave from his dreams, if he ever gets some free time, and I think the entity from hell had better watch out. Dave doesn't scare easily.

Update: As we were in the process of writing this book Dave had another dream related to this mysterious cave by the river. In late April of 2003 Dave again had a dream related to the ominous cave near his house. This time there was a new twist to the dream. This time the dream started and he found himself walking alone down a path that went through a forest. On his left was the Elkhorn river and on the right he saw the riverbanks, covered with trees. He then heard a rumbling noise, like a stampede that swelled and grew ever closer. Suddenly, hundreds of thousands of deer crested a hill and came running frantically by him. He had to jump quickly off the path to get out of the way of the stampeding deer. After the deer had passed by, he got back onto the path and came upon the cave that was surrounded by trees and bushes. As he started heading for the cave he abruptly woke up.

Dave's impression of this unusual dream was that the deer were running because they were obviously scared of something and it would make sense that it would have been the evil presence in the cave. Something struck fear into the hearts of the deer, causing them to run for their lives.

Chapter 5

Ball Cemetery

Dave met Leslie after he had been researching the paranormal on the Internet for some time but he didn't want to tell her right away about his interest in the paranormal for fear of scaring her off. He was afraid that she would think he was a little off in the head. After they got to know each other better, Dave decided the timing was right and he would take her someplace. The first place he wanted to show her was Ball Cemetery in central Nebraska. He had only been dating her for a few months and went to pick her up one day for a date and he asked her " if he could take her *some place unusual*." Not exactly sure what he meant by "unusual," she was reluctant but finally agreed to go.

Leslie picked up the account here and recounted that they arrived at Ball Cemetery after dark and it was a very bright moon that night. The cemetery was, "one of the spookiest places I've ever been and it looked like one of those places in a 60's werewolf movie." The cemetery was lined with tall trees and the moon shimmering off of the headstones made plenty of creepy shadows. It gave her the creeps, but they walked around to check it out as Dave took some pictures. Then they walked outside the cemetery for a while and they were standing at the fence when suddenly Leslie was kicked in the shin by some unseen entity. She didn't see anything at the time but certainly felt the kick and had a large bruise the next day to prove it. Odd.

Eager to see if anything unusual turned up on the pictures, they excitedly dropped them off at the 1-hour photo at K-Mart the following day. When they returned and picked up the finished pictures they were very surprised at what they were looking at. They had some incredible photos with ghostly apparitions that they couldn't explain. In addition, Leslie had a huge bruise on her shin to bolster her own belief.

This is one of the first pictures that Dave and Leslie took in Ball Cemetery in Nebraska. The unnatural shape cannot be explained logically.

Dave first ran across Ball Cemetery in central Nebraska in his high school years. He grew up around there and in 1973-1974, Dave and some friends would take their dates to the cemetery in an attempt to, "scare them and play huggy-huggy" as he put it. He went on to say, "When I was out there the first time, I saw people walking around, yet we were the only ones there! I'd get a glimpse of someone walking down a road or by a tree. I knew something was going on but I didn't know exactly what."

After he had taken Leslie there and she was kicked on the leg by some unseen entity and their unusual pictures were developed they knew they had to go back and take some more pictures. They have countless numbers of photographs with unusual anomalies, anomalies that they believe are ghosts. After making a few trips out there by themselves, Dave and Leslie took some friends of theirs along with them the next time. Kel and Darby were initially very skeptical but they soon discovered that the photos they took also had some very unusual anomalies. Kel and Darby were intrigued by the photos and the idea of ghost hunting had starting to grow on them. The race was on to find some answers and continue this quest for knowledge of the supernatural.

They spent a long time, after these first encounters, returning to Ball Cemetery taking pictures and talking to the spirits. Initially, they felt very uneasy there. Some of the first pictures had frightening images and they felt the spirits there were trying to scare them off. However, they returned during the daylight hours and helped out by picking up trash, beer bottles and set headstones upright that had been knocked over by vandals if they were physically able to. They repaired quite a few of the headstones. That evening the group returned after dark and the atmosphere in the cemetery was completely different than the previous several visits. Instead of being threatening or hostile, Dave recalls that it was more like, "sitting outside in your own yard at night." It was much more comfortable than the previous visits. He knew that there were many entities around that they couldn't see, watching them, but the act of helping out at the cemetery seemed to let the spirits know that the Paranormal Investigations team meant them no disrespect.

On all of the visits to Ball Cemetery they had the distinct feeling that they were being watched. One entity in particular they nicknamed, "The Walker" because he would always be walking around the cemetery. This entity would watch them from a distance, walking from tree to tree along the fence line, always keeping his distance. He always stayed close enough to watch them but far enough away that the entity didn't think they would see him.

On one trip there Leslie was walking in front of Dave with an electromagnetic field tester meter (EMF meter for short.) This is a technique that they use for taking pictures. One person walks with the EMF meter and when they get a reading showing abnormal field activity, the other person takes a picture. Many times they will get unusual pictures when they use this technique. While they were walking through the cemetery with the EMF meter and camera at the ready Dave heard a voice call his full name, "David." The only person he lets call him David is his wife because he hates being called David. Dave asked Leslie what she wanted but she hadn't said anything. Thinking that maybe it was his imagination, he continued on and about ten minutes later he heard it again. "David," the voice called. This time he was sure he heard it and he knew it was coming from behind him. He quickly turned around to see a ball of light floating in midair behind him. Not only was it a ball of light but it was in the shape of a woman's head! This really freaked Dave out as you can imagine. He was scared, but not quite scared enough to run just yet. He was paralyzed with fear for an instant and before he could move, the head quickly floated off and vanished. He excitedly yelled to Leslie to ask her if she had seen the floating woman's head but she hadn't so they continued walking through the cemetery looking for unusual readings on the EMF meter.

A few minutes later, Leslie was getting unusually high readings with the EMF meter and looked up to see the same, glowing, floating woman's head directly in front of her, looking at her. Leslie stood there in awe (and some fear I suspect) staring at this apparition and, again, it quickly floated away and vanished in an instant.

A few weeks later, Dave and Leslie returned to Ball Cemetery and Dave couldn't stop thinking about the floating head he saw there on his previous visit. The name Mary stuck in Dave's mind and he had a very strong feeling that her name was Mary. As he walked through the cemetery, he suddenly smelled a very sweet honeysuckle perfume. He asked Leslie if she could smell it as she was standing right behind him but she couldn't detect any scent and she wasn't wearing perfume. Dave then grabbed Leslie, took a quick step backwards and moved Leslie to the spot where he was just standing and she did then smell the honeysuckle perfume for a fleeting moment before it dissipated in the open air. They continued to walk through the cemetery and a few minutes later Dave felt someone pulling on his ponytail and he heard a woman giggling. It was like a high school girl teasing her boyfriend. From that point on, every time they returned to the cemetery if Dave didn't say, "Hi, Mary" when he entered the cemetery the unseen entity would pull his ponytail and giggle.

On a subsequent visit to Ball Cemetery, Dave and Leslie were talking to some kids and heard of a local boy who went to Millard High School. A week prior to this visit several kids were partying, drinking and "raising hell" when one boy decided that he was going to go into the cemetery and be Joe Cool. He said he wasn't afraid of any ghosts and proceeded to go into the cemetery and kick over some headstones. Then he pretended that he was being beaten up and all the other kids thought that it was pretty funny. A moment later the kid in the cemetery fell down and was yelling for help and the other kids kind of laughed again, thinking their drunken buddy was hamming it up some more. The rest of the kids entered the cemetery to see what (for confidentiality we'll call him Bob) Bob was up to. The other boys suddenly became very concerned to see that Bob had been beaten up pretty badly by someone, or something. Bob was beaten unconscious and was hospitalized for several days for his injuries. Dave and Leslie spoke with the boy and his parents after the incident and confirmed his account of being beaten by some unseen entity. Bob and his parents have the medical records to prove his account, or at least that he was hospitalized for some serious injuries. Bob now believes in ghosts and will certainly show more respect for the dead the next time he sets foot anywhere near a cemetery!

Dave and Leslie were there about a week after Bob had been beaten up and made their way to the cemetery to see what they could find. Dave suspects that the entity they nicknamed, "The Walker" would know what happened to Bob because he is always lurking around, watching what goes on in the cemetery. They feel that "The Walker" is or may be the guardian of the cemetery and may even be responsible for Bob's injuries.

It was after dusk and Dave and Leslie were standing in the center of the cemetery. Dave was looking down a row of trees and could see something moving at the end of it. It started moving closer when Dave then realized that the entity was indeed The Walker. When The Walker got to within twenty-five feet of Dave, it suddenly stopped and looked up and to the right so Dave quickly took a picture of it, seizing the opportunity. It then looked back down towards Dave and started moving towards him again, closing fast. The only thing Dave could think to do was to quickly put his arms down to his sides as a sign of submission and to let The Walker know that he didn't intend to cause any problems. Dave was hoping that The Walker didn't intend to cause him any problems either! As the entity got closer to Dave it faded away and he could feel it either passing through him or around him. Dave suddenly got a cold chill that actually took his breath away for a brief moment and then it passed.

The next day, they had the pictures developed and the picture that Dave had taken of The Walker from close distance came out very clear. The entity was looking up over his right shoulder. On the bottom left side of the picture you can see the gravestone of Mary Mumford. Coming up out of the grave there appears to be ectoplasm. They believe the ectoplasm captured on film was Mary Mumford. Dave strongly feels that the spirit of Mary Mumford intervened and saved them from possible bodily harm from The Walker.

Apparently, teenagers learn the hard way. On another evening as Dave and Leslie were making their way to the cemetery for further investigation, they noticed a carload of boys leaving the cemetery rather quickly, passing them in the parking lot, flying down the windy road out of there. As Dave and Leslie entered the cemetery, they noticed some headstones looked like they had recently been knocked over. Several minutes later, four boys came walking slowly up the road, the same boys who had moments earlier been heading the other way in a big hurry. Dave and Leslie met the boys outside the cemetery gates in the parking lot where the boys confessed to knocking over some headstones. They were scared because as they were flying down the road away from the cemetery, the brakes on their car suddenly went out and the boys ended up in a ditch. None of the boys were injured but they certainly were shaken up. The boys suspected a supernatural connection to their car troubles and they may have been right!

Dave sternly lectured the boys on respecting grave sites and cemeteries. He asked them how they would feel if someone desecrated the grave of one of their relatives, parents or loved one and they understood and seemed genuinely sorry for being so disrespectful. Dave told them they needed to go back into the cemetery and fix the headstones they knocked over and apologize to the spirits for being so disrespectful. Only one of them had actually knocked over the headstones and the others were just with him. As the four entered the cemetery to repair the damage, one of them could not move past the main gate. He physically was being held back by some unseen force. The other three kids encountered no resistance and quickly righted the headstones and apologized to the spirits as instructed by Dave.

The boys then left again, promising never to be disrespectful to the dead again. They were firm believers in the supernatural after what they had just witnessed. They walked back to their car, which was still in the ditch and they managed to push it out after some effort. As they drove back into town their car again went into the ditch. None of the boys were hurt in this second accident of the night but they were downright scared and feared for their safety! They have stayed in contact since this incident with Dave and Leslie through e-mail and have expressed genuine remorse for what they did. The boys have promised to respect the dead and to let all of their friends know that it's not OK to do what they did. The boy who actually kicked the headstones over is very scared for his safety. He now knows that the spirit world is a powerful thing and not to be taken lightly or toyed with. None of the team members at Paranormal Investigations think that this boy will ever set foot again in a cemetery until he is laid to rest himself!

One unique thing that Dave and Leslie do is go to the cemetery with a small TV set and radio. They talk to the spirits and update them on what's going on in the outside world. In doing so they feel they've created a bond between themselves and the current residents of Ball Cemetery. To an outside observer this may seem a little eccentric but if you look at it from the perspective that maybe they're right and the spirits can see and understand them, it makes perfect sense. After all, the spirit world is eager to keep up on current events just like anyone else.

Many times when Dave and Leslie would be there by themselves investigating the cemetery, local kids would start up the road at night towards the cemetery. The kids would usually come to the cemetery to party, drink and fool around so one night Dave came up with a clever idea. As the cars neared the cemetery, Dave took a picture and when the flash went off the cars stopped in their tracks. A moment later, they started towards the cemetery again and Dave took another picture but this time the cars turned around and made a hasty retreat. They didn't return that evening.

Halloween soon came around and seeing how well the flash scared the kids away, Dave came up with another idea that was sure to scare the pants off the local teenagers. He decided to take his Halloween skull mask and black duster up with them for their next investigation, just in case. Like clockwork, the carloads of kids pulled into the cemetery parking lot just outside the gates on Halloween as the Paranormal Investigations team was there investigating the cemetery. Dave was determined to "scare the daylights" out of some kids who were up to no good. He stood behind a tree and the other team members hid behind some headstones. Just as the car headlights brushed across the dark cemetery, Dave stepped out from behind the tree so the headlights would illuminate him for a brief second. Immediately after that, the only noise that could be heard was screaming coming from the car that had just lit up Dave with the headlights. There were girls' voices screaming so loud that dogs were running miles away, and the boys were screaming, "Get out of here, get out of here!" in frantic adolescent voices. The cars left the cemetery so fast that they went down the windy road away from the cemetery never using their brakes once, which was quite remarkable.

Chapter 6

The Omaha Entity

The Christensen's phone rang and on the other end was Lisa (last name withheld for privacy) from Omaha. Lisa said that, "There is something in my house and it's been here for quite a while, but it's started to become frightening." It was shaking the house, making horrible smells, waking her up at night and she was getting very frightened.

Dave and Leslie went to Lisa's house to talk to her and look over the house. Lisa said she had been in the house for seven years and the haunting started about two years prior to her calling Dave and Leslie. The incidents started out to be scary but almost amusing at the same time. The entity started out by playing with Lisa's daughter's crayons, bouncing them on the table and making noise, flipping lights off and on and changing the radio stations. Lisa would actually talk to the entity and play games with it and she didn't seem too concerned at first. It was her daughter's imaginary "friend." Things were initially pretty mellow.

On several occasions when Lisa would be coming up to the door with her arms full of groceries, the entity would actually unlock and open the door for her.

On other occasions, as a full-time student, Lisa would frequently have papers out and around the computer. There would also be stacks of papers due at any given time. On several occasions Lisa went to work only to return home and find her papers neatly sorted and stacked, right where she needed them. How was this possible?

Another time it was believed that the entity wrote on the daughter's bedroom wall with crayons and Lisa told it not to do that because it was bad. The next day she went into the same room to find that there was now writing on the screen by the window. The entity had listened and didn't write on the wall again!

One cold October, there was a heavy, wet snow in Omaha and it knocked out the power to large areas of the city. Lisa was one of the unlucky people without power and the house started to get cold fast. The entity could be heard in the basement banging on the side of the furnace, trying desperately to get it going again. Apparently, it didn't understand that you need electricity to run the furnace.

One night Lisa was giving her daughter a bath and the entity came up behind her and pulled on her shirt, scaring her. It had never done that before and she was startled by this incident. She yelled at it and told it that was "inappropriate behavior" and to not do that. This made things with the entity worse, much worse. Lisa had initially called the Christensens after this incident occurred, when things turned bad very quickly.

Notice the orb near the peak in the attic.

The Christensens made about six more visits to the house to gather information on the case. During the course of the initial investigation they found out that Lisa had gotten pregnant but made the choice not to keep the baby. She was an unwed mother going to school full-time and she was also a full-time nurse. She just felt it wasn't the proper time to have a child so she had an abortion. It was a few months after the abortion that the odd things around the house started to happen. Lisa's decision to have the abortion without consulting her boyfriend caused the couple to break up. He was very upset that she hadn't consulted him at all regarding the decision to have the abortion and he left her.

During the course of the investigation, Dave and Leslie received a call from Fox 42 News. They wanted to do a story on them (Paranormal Investigations) and Lisa agreed, as long as they didn't show her face or use her name or address and Fox agreed not to disclose Lisa's identity or address.

While Fox 42 was at Lisa's house filming for the segment, Dave and Leslie decided to introduce the reporter and the cameraman to the entity that they nicknamed Adrian. The photographer had been through the entire house taking pictures. Dave and Leslie told the photographer and the reporter to come upstairs and meet Adrian. Adrian would hide in the attic in a crawl space behind a wall that Dave and Leslie could not get to. Leslie told the reporter to go ahead and sit down. The reporter felt silly talking to something she couldn't see and Leslie piped up, "It's OK, we always feel silly like we're talking to nothing." The reporter then stuck her hand into the crawl space area and told Adrian that it was OK, she was a friend and he could hold her hand. She suddenly looked up, shocked, and said, "Oh my God, he touched me, he's holding my hand!" she was quite excited that the entity was touching her hand. She could actually feel the pressure like someone was holding her hand but nothing was there. Nothing that you could see anyway.

After the interview was over the cameraman wanted to get a close-out segment showing the long steps going up to the attic and he was going to fade out when he got to the attic. The first time he started up the stairs filming and he was almost to the top when his camera suddenly shut off. Puzzled, he retreated to try again and the second time he made it about half way up the stairs when the camera shut off. Frustrated, he retreated again. On the third try he didn't even make it to the stairs when the camera shut off. Clearly frustrated, he turned to the Christensens and said, "Please, tell this little entity to quit playing with the camera so I can get my work done." They all kind of joked about it and Leslie then told Adrian to "leave the cameraman alone so he can get his work done." The cameraman turned his camera back on and slowly walked up the stairs again, this time without incident. When the reporter and cameraman walked out of the house a few minutes later, they were two firm believers in the spirit world. When they had first arrived however, they were very skeptical.

The segment was taped and aired around October of 1997 and Lisa's ex-boyfriend saw the segment and decided to call Lisa and see how she was doing. They ended up dating again and things went well for them. As a matter of fact, things went so well for them, about six months after dating again Lisa and her ex-boyfriend, who was now her boyfriend again, decided to get married. During this entire time the entity was still in her house and causing some mischief.

Lisa and her boyfriend married shortly afterwards and within four months of being married Lisa found out she was pregnant. Within six weeks of finding out she was pregnant the haunting suddenly stopped entirely. The entity has left her alone and has not returned.

Some of the antics encountered during the investigation in Lisa's house were amusing and it appeared to have a sense of humor. Frequently, the entity would move furniture around, turn the stereo on and off and change stations. On one occasion, Lisa's sister was spending the night in the basement and she was ready for bed. Lisa's sister climbed into bed and reached up to turn the stand up floor lamp off when it suddenly went off by itself before she had even touched the switch! She then discovered that the cord had been unplugged from the wall.

She was scared so badly that she couldn't sleep downstairs and ended up sleeping upstairs on the couch. She then left the next day even though she had intended to stay the weekend. She was simply too scared to stay there another night!

In speaking with Lisa's young daughter, the child said that "her friend" would sometimes make her nervous. Sometimes he would not play nice with her toys and it made her nervous when he would bounce her Etch-A-Sketch up and down and make the picture disappear.

While the investigation was ongoing, the Christensen's told Lisa that if she wanted to get the entity out of her home they would see what they could do. The other option was to have Lisa apologize to the entity for yelling at it and just deal with the situation, assuming it didn't become violent. Lisa opted for this option and apologized to "Adrian" and things did in fact calm down. Lisa would get home from work and loudly announce, "Mom's home!" including "Adrian" in the welcome and at no time after this up until he left was he violent.

The entity left entirely after she found out she was pregnant and has not returned.

Dave and Leslie have a theory about this haunting. They believe that the entity was the spirit of a child because of the childlike behavior it showed. They also feel that when Lisa yelled at it, it became somewhat violent because it is the spirit of a child and this is how children react to being scolded. They throw a tantrum. The last part of the theory sounds strange to many people but it does make sense. They believe that the entity could have been the spirit of the child she had aborted. After all, the haunting didn't start until after she had the abortion and it stopped completely after she became pregnant again. They believe that the entity may have waited around so the couple could get back together and it could be born and have another shot at life as we know it.

Another interesting note to this case. About eight months after Lisa and her boyfriend broke up, the ex-boyfriend put flowers on her car one day in an attempt to make up. Suddenly, the whole house started to shake and Lisa could hear footsteps running back and forth above her head and the window started rattling. She then went to the window to see why it was rattling and she spotted the flowers on the hood of her car. Adrian had been trying to get Lisa's attention and it worked.

The entity had been actually friendly and playful until Lisa had yelled at it on the one occasion and that appears to be what set it off. It had generally looked out for Lisa prior to that. On some occasions, if someone were up by the house the entity would slam a door or window or do something to get Lisa's attention. It seemed to be protective of Lisa and her daughter.

Now the house is again peaceful. Adrian has apparently left for good and the couple is happily married. This case had a happy ending all the way around.

Chapter 7

The Love Triangle

The love triangle resulted in paranormal activity with some incredible power. This case took place in South Omaha, Nebraska. Gail and her husband had a two-year old child and one day she walked out on her husband and moved in with a new boyfriend that she had recently met. Her husband was in the Air Force and worked at Offutt Air Force Base in Omaha, Nebraska. He was a very jealous, possessive type and was filled with rage at the sudden turn of events.

One night after his wife had left him, he found her and her new boyfriend at a local bar and confronted them with a gun outside in the parking lot. The Sheriff was called to break it up and the husband was arrested and thrown in jail. When he got out, he was mad as hell and went over to the boyfriend's house where his estranged wife, Gail, was living with their daughter. He knocked on the door and the boyfriend's mother, who also lived at the house, saw the estranged husband and recognized him immediately. Gail had a restraining order against him and he was not supposed to be anywhere near her or his daughter. Unfortunately, they didn't have a phone in the house. The boyfriend's mother made the mistake of opening the door just a crack and the estranged husband forced his way into the house. An argument ensued and the boyfriend's mother grabbed Gail's child and ran next door to call the police.

While next door, the boyfriend's mother could hear the argument in full swing and then she heard a gunshot. Next she heard the estranged husband yell, "Oh my God, what did I do?" This was immediately followed by another gunshot. Then there was silence.

The police quickly arrived and found Gail dead with a gunshot to the head. The estranged husband was also dead from a fatal gunshot wound.

The couple's small daughter was later sent to live with the wife's family and is currently doing well.

Dave received a call from a man living near 33rd and L Street in South Omaha. He told Dave about something strange going on in his house. He said doors would open and slam shut, and cupboard doors would rapidly open and close by themselves. He said that the only time that this would happen is when he and his wife would get into arguments. Otherwise it was fairly quiet around the house. The man who called Dave was the boyfriend's father. The house is where the murder and suicide occurred and the boyfriend's father still owns and lives in the house.

Dave and Leslie arrived and knew what had happened in the house. They had done their usual research and certainly suspected the murder/suicide may be responsible for the current paranormal activity that was reported.

The first thing they did was to walk around the house with tape recorders and ask some fairly simple questions. "Who are you? Why are you here? This simple technique will sometimes capture ghostly voices on tape and help to unravel the mystery. It doesn't always work but it's a good investigative tool. This technique is widely used by paranormal investigators to search for unusual activity. Normally, if it works at all, the ghostly voices will only be heard when the tape is played back.

To see if they had any success, after a few minutes they went outside and played the tape back. What they heard made their skin crawl! They heard a woman's voice, crying and asking for help. The voice cried out, "Help! Help me, help me!" The boyfriend's father who owns the house was also outside and listened to the tape and suddenly grew very pale. He looked up at Dave and Leslie and said, "That's Gail, that's Gail's voice! I know her voice, that's her!"

The team had also taken several pictures while in the house on the initial visit. After they got the initial pictures developed Dave and Leslie returned to the house where the tragedy occurred. Now they knew the identity of the entity in the house; it was Gail. After hearing the ghostly woman's voice on the tape and seeing the boyfriend's father's reaction, there was no doubt that the entity was Gail. After all, it made sense. What about the estranged husband? Was there more than one entity in this house?

They returned with the tape recorders and asked, "What can we do for you? How can we help you?" They didn't get any response on tape this time. While they were there they took several more pictures in various rooms of the house to see if they could capture any unusual activity.

They again left and had the new pictures developed the next day. They found in the room where the murder-suicide occurred there were actually two entities that were caught on film. Dave and Leslie immediately thought that the two entities were obviously Gail and her estranged husband. They knew from the tape that the one entity was Gail. It seemed logical that the jealous estranged husband would remain there too. He remained as jealous in death as he had been in life.

After seeing the photos showing two entities in the living room they returned to the house again armed with an electro-magnetic field tester meter (EMF meter) this time. In order to make sure the electricity didn't interfere with their equipment, they turned off the main breaker. Dave then checked the EMF meter and was able to determine that only Gail's entity was in the room with him and the meter read 32.8. This is an extremely high reading for a house with no electricity on. A normal EMF meter reading when the power is off would be 0.0. Shortly thereafter, the reading on the EMF meter spiked up over 72 and they immediately knew that there was another entity in the room with them. They certainly weren't alone! Dave started talking to Gail and reassured her that, "He can't hurt you now. You're not a physical form anymore. No matter what he does, he can't hurt you and he can't harm you. He's just holding you here because he knows that if he let's go, you're going to be free and he's going to have to face the consequences of what he did so don't be afraid of him. Let him know that he can't hurt you." Dave spoke to Gail that way for about forty-five minutes, at one point telling her to go to the light. Suddenly, the readings dropped by half on the EMF meter. One of the entities had left. It was Gail who had left, leaving Dave, Leslie and two women who are friends of the family in the room with one very angry, jealous spirit of Gail's estranged husband.

Without warning, there was a very loud roar throughout the entire house and a big gust of wind started swirling around the living room. The door leading outdoors suddenly slammed shut by itself. They were all a little nervous and decided maybe it was best to leave the room for a minute to gather their thoughts and the group quickly headed for the other door. It quickly slammed shut and they couldn't get it open to save their skins! They were now effectively trapped inside the living room of the house. The roar and rumbling noise continued to resonate through the house. Dave described the sound as being like, "The roar of a lion along with the rumbling of a jet engine and it just shook the house."

Dave's usually the crazy one who does all the talking and bickering with the entities and he went to the middle of the room and announced to the remaining entity, "You can't bother us. You can't hurt us. There's nothing that you're going to do that's going to hurt us. You have no power over us, you have no power anymore so just release the doors and go away. You're not welcome here anymore. Gail's not here anymore and you have no reason to be here so just leave." Dave continued on for about ten to fifteen minutes stating his point but heard no response from the entity. Dave continued to tell the entity to leave. Suddenly, the foul smell left the room, the roar and the rumbling noise stopped and the coldness went away just as quickly as it started.

It was ninety-five degrees outside but inside the room where they were trapped it was so cold that they could literally see their breath. It was a cold that would chill you to the bone. This type of coldness is very often associated with paranormal activity. The room was so cold that they were all shivering, even though it was sweltering hot outside. The two women friends of the family were terrified at the events that had unfolded in front of them. One of them was bawling and the other was trying to comfort her, even though she was terrified herself.

The two women witnesses apparently thought that Dave and Leslie were going to perform some type of sleight of hand and were not believers in the paranormal. They certainly left that house with a different impression than they came in with!

After the second entity left the house they were able to easily open the doors and they all rushed out of the house into the back yard. The two women witnesses bolted from the house into the farthest corner of the back yard and the one who was hysterical in the house collapsed in a heap, sobbing. Several of the neighbors had come over because they had heard the unearthly rumbling and roaring noises and were trying to figure out what was going on. Dave explained to the owner of the house what had just happened and the owner went into the house to check it out for himself. He told Dave that he could immediately tell the difference in the atmosphere. It was now a very comfortable feeling.

After speaking with the homeowner and digging into details that led up to the haunting, the homeowner had shown Dave and Leslie where the bodies from the tragic murder/suicide had been found. He also stated how he had to clean up the blood that was all over the floor and that it had run into the heating vent on the floor but he hadn't taken that out and cleaned it. Dave said that any time there are any bodily fluids spilled or splashed on the property, especially blood, from a traumatic event such as a murder that it tends to hold the negative energy in the area. The traumatic murder itself was enough to stir up some paranormal activity but to have the dried blood in the vent would aggravate the situation even more.

A few months after the big showdown with the entities, Dave called the homeowner to see how things were going and all was well. The homeowner would occasionally get into an argument with his wife and nothing unusual would occur so he knew that Gail and her estranged husband had finally left. He could still feel the difference in the atmosphere of the house and knew that they were still gone. Hopefully, Gail went to the light and the estranged husband went anywhere, as long as he had left the house!

Chapter 8

Grandma's Still Here

Dave received a call from Becky in Omaha in the central part of the city around 60th and Blando. She was a twenty-one-year-old mother of two children. Tom was six years old and David was six months old at the time the investigation started. She called Dave and Leslie after a bizarre incident with her youngest son, David.

Becky had gone downstairs to do some laundry and had forgotten to shut the basement door. After she switched the laundry she turned around to go back upstairs and was horrified to see her youngest son David standing at the top of the stairs. Before she could do anything, David took a step forward and fell. She panicked for obvious reasons, as it appeared David was going to tumble down the stairs. Becky told Dave that David, "Floated from the top of the stairs to the bottom of the stairs and was gently laid on the basement floor."

Dave found the story to be "quite incredible" but also thought it definitely needed to be checked out. They made an appointment for May 14th of 1997 to meet and this would allow Dave and Leslie to take some meter readings around the house. They arrived at the modest, ranch-style house and noted that toys were scattered all around and the yard was in bad shape. Inside, the house was pretty messy. The children seemed to be OK and they didn't see any signs of abuse or neglect. They interviewed Becky and then took some meter

51

readings around various locations in the house with the EMF meter described in the previous chapters. They did get some unusually high readings in portions of the house and this got their curiosity up. They would enter the rooms and the readings would be unusually high and then they would suddenly drop. Whatever was there apparently left the rooms as they entered.

They interviewed Becky and found that she was a high school dropout but fairly intelligent. She grew up in a somewhat hostile environment. Her parents didn't get along very well. She had brothers and seemed to get along very well with them. As Dave and Leslie looked through the rooms they kept an eye out for any signs of drug-related items or drugs, thinking this could be the cause. They also keep an eye out for any signs of alcohol abuse. In some cases people get high or drunk and hallucinate and the ghost turns out to be the result of a joint or maybe some Jack Daniels.

Dave then spoke with the older son, Tom, who told Dave about his make believe friend who he would play with down in the basement in the back room. He said they would play for hours and he would sit in this closet area and talk to the make believe friend. His mother would frequently ask who he was talking to, but he would not answer her most of the time. Dave asked Tom who his make believe friend was and he looked at Dave and said, "Grandma." Becky had a stunned look on her face. Tom continued and added that, "Grandma stays in the closet beneath the front porch and grandma won't come out unless it's nighttime." She'll come out to play with them at night and Tom will go into the closet and play with her during the day. They then sent Tom to play by himself while Dave, Leslie and Becky went upstairs to discuss the information they just extracted from Tom. It turns out that the grandmother passed away a month prior to the birth of Tom. Before she passed away she told Becky that she was quite upset and sad because she wouldn't get to see and spend time with her grandchild. Becky then stated that there were a number of strange things that would happen around the house, like strange noises and flashes of light but she really hadn't paid attention to them. The kids had apparently kept Becky too busy to notice the paranormal activity that was occurring around the house.

On a hunch, Dave asked Becky if Tom had ever seen any photographs of his deceased grandmother. She thought about it a minute and then replied that he hadn't. She had photo albums in the basement but she had never shown him pictures of her and he had never seen her. He then asked her to get some of the albums out. She ventured into the basement and when she returned she had found two of the photo albums and proceeded to show Dave the works, going into great detail regarding the subjects, events and dates. Finally, they came to a photograph showing four middle-aged women. One of them was Becky's mother, two were Becky's sisters and the third was a family friend. Dave then asked Becky if they could show the picture to Tom and see if he could really pick out Grandma, like an improvised police lineup. Dave said, "Lets give it a shot and see if he really sees Grandma." Becky was doubtful, as she insisted that Tom had never seen a picture of her.

Becky called Tom upstairs and he bounded up the stairs and into the room where they were looking at the photo album. Dave then asked Tom, "Tom, do you know anybody in this picture?" He looked at the picture and excitedly replied, "Grandma!" He then pointed at his deceased grandmother in the photo. At this point, Dave thought Becky might just faint judging by the look on her pale face!

Becky, Dave and Leslie continued the interview to see what other details might now emerge. Becky thought back and recalled other odd things that had happened. About 10:30 p.m. Becky put David to bed in his crib. Like many cribs, she had a musical mobile over the crib to calm him and help him get to sleep. Dave and Leslie set a table up just outside of David's door so they could monitor his room for any unusual activity. They continued their conversation with Becky. They could hear David in there giggling and playing but other than that, he was quiet. Then suddenly his mobile started to play at about 11:30 p.m. Odd, David couldn't even reach it and nobody else was in the room with him, at least no one that was living.

They all proceeded to David's room to see what was going on. As they approached the bedroom door they could still hear the mobile chiming out the children's tune. The second they opened the door it abruptly stopped. David also stopped giggling. He was wide-awake. He was also only six months old and not able to stand up and wind up the mobile. How did it start then? They proceeded into the room and took some additional electromagnetic field meter (EMF) readings in various parts of the room. When they had first arrived and checked this particular room the highest reading on the EMF meter was 5.6, which is high to begin with. Now, the room was noticeably much cooler and the EMF meter readings were 27.8, very high. There was something in the room that was causing the meter readings to skyrocket and the room to cool like a walk-in freezer! There was no appliance or electronic source close enough to drive the EMF meter readings up that high. Thinking that this was a very good sign that paranormal activity was in progress, Dave and Leslie started taking pictures throughout the house.

The next day, they made their ritual trek to the one-hour photo shop at K-Mart to get their pictures developed. They anxiously waited the hour much like a child waits for Santa on Christmas Eve. They promptly claimed their pictures and quickly reviewed their work. Much to their excitement, they did get several shots of orbs, proving that paranormal activity was present when they took the pictures. Then they got to the picture of Tom. He had proudly stated that he wanted his picture taken with Grandma and that she was there with them in the room. They had complied with his request and took Tom's picture the evening before and as they came to it, they were very surprised at what they found. In between Dave and Leslie and Tom was Grandma, only she wasn't looking very human. The picture showed an image that showed Tom and a vortex or image that looked very much like a tornado of light. The image was stunning and showed that there was a great deal of energy in the room.

Becky was quite upset by these developments. She was very upset by the fact that there were indeed entities in her house. In addition to her mother there were some other entities that they didn't know the identities of yet.

Now very much interested, Dave and Leslie did some investigative work regarding the background of the house. They were surprised to find that the house was built entirely of used lumber, steel and bricks from an old church that was torn down in North Omaha. There was nothing unusual with the property itself. The area around the house had been farmland only seventy years prior. They could find nothing unusual about the property but were very much thinking that the building materials may be contributing to the haunting. Dave explained that spirits are attracted to places of worship and just because the old church was torn down, that didn't mean it had been forgotten. Spirits like to linger in places of worship and when old churches are torn down and recycled like that, the spirits tend to linger or stay with the material, which just now happened to be Becky's home. It seems the spirits feel a certain attachment to the structure of the old church and they just aren't quite ready to leave yet.

About two months after they completed their investigation at Becky's, Dave and Leslie stopped by to check on things. Grandma was still there and Tom continued to play with her in the basement under the stairs. It seems that she is now a little more at ease about coming out during the day and Tom not only played with her under the stairs in the basement but also in his bedroom, kitchen, living room or wherever she was. They were almost inseparable. Wherever Grandma was, Tom was. He would carry on full-blown conversations with her and would even mediate between Grandma and Becky.

The situation is the same with David and Grandma still plays with him too.

As for Becky, she has grown accustomed to the idea that her mother still lives with her, along with the other entities. She isn't bothered anymore by the fact that she shares her home with ghosts. She doesn't feel threatened by them and has learned to accept the fact that the family has gotten just a little bit larger.

Chapter 9

The House on Haunted Hill

In the summer of 2000 Dave began to have constant dreams about a house that sat on top of a hill. It was really an old house that had a large, newer addition. To get to the house, you had to drive down a windy dirt road, going up and down some hills and through a forest to get to the house. As you entered the old part of the house you would quickly find that it was haunted. Down in the basement there was an underground river with a very fast current. When you looked out from the house you could see another river out in the distance, with rising hills behind the river. It always bothered Dave. It was one of those things that he wanted to find out more about. Did this place exist? Why was he constantly having these dreams? Always more questions than answers.

All of the trouble and gangs in Omaha had made Dave and Leslie think about moving to the country where they would have some peace and quiet and some space to relax in. Dave was searching the Internet looking for homes somewhat close to Omaha when he came across the photo of the home they now live in. He knew he had to go see that particular house, now. Leslie couldn't go with Dave to look at the house right then so he decided to go on a road trip himself to see if he could even find it. He did. It was a nice, raised, ranch-style house. He spoke to the woman who owned it and he thought it was nice and it came with seven acres of land! He went outside and when he was getting into his truck he looked to the East and could see a scenic valley with lots of trees and the river off in the distance. Behind the river were some hills with limestone bluffs. It was a beautiful view, he thought. He called Leslie and told her that this was a "must see" place. He told her he really wanted it and it was in a nice area. It did need to be cleaned up and it needed some repairs but that didn't matter. Leslie went out there with Dave as they met the real estate agent and looked over the place again. They decided right away they would buy it and they did in September of 2000.

October of 2000 finally arrived and the Christensens started to move into their new home. The moving crew consisted of Dave and Leslie, Dave's two sons and grandson, Leslie's son and a few other friends. Leslie went ahead of Dave with an armload of things to be carried in and proceeded up the stairs followed closely by Dave. Dave suddenly had a very overpowering feeling that something very bad was following him up the stairs and didn't really want him there. He quickly turned around but saw nothing. He then told his wife, "Leslie, there's something in this house." She replied, "No, it's just your imagination." But Dave insisted, "No, there's somebody in this house!"

That night, Dave's grandson Conner, his two boys and a few of their friends stayed in the new house. Everyone likes a new house and they were excited to be staying there and the boys took over the basement. Late that evening Dave's two sons and his friends were spooked by something in the basement and made their way upstairs to finish sleeping, leaving Conner alone in the basement asleep on the couch.

The next morning after everyone got up and about, Conner made his way up from the basement. He went up to Dave and nonchalantly said, "Grandpa, you've got a haunted house!" Dave was shocked, but quickly remembered his feeling as he was walking up the stairs while moving in and he turned to Leslie and said, "I told you." Leslie wanted to know more about why Conner thought the house was haunted. She asked him, "What do you mean?" Conner replied with the candor that any child will show. "You have a ghost. She's a pretty lady and she has big boobies." Great, Dave thought, just what I need.

As time went on, the entity gave Dave a very weird, creepy feeling. He had the distinct feeling that whatever was there in the basement didn't want him there, in his or her space. He couldn't shake that feeling.

Dave's boys met some new friends and they were going to stay over at their house one evening. After his boys had left Dave decided to make an announcement to whatever entities were in the house and would listen. He told them, "I know you're here and I know you don't particularly care for me, but I'm staying and I'm going to lay down some rules.

"Rule number one, stay away from my boys. You don't show yourselves to them, you don't go in their rooms and you stay away from them.

"Rule number two, you stay out of our room, you do not go in there whatsoever.

"Rule number three, if you show yourself to us, let us know you're here first because I do not like surprises."

After finding out their new house was haunted, Dave and Leslie did a little research to see if they could find out why it was haunted and maybe who was haunting it. The family that the Christensens purchased the home from had lost the father to a car accident about a year before they sold the house. The children reported to the wife after the tragic accident that they had seen their deceased father in the house. Now things started to make sense. They had purchased the home at a really great price. They were able to purchase the home and seven acres of land for around $125,000 when the value at that time should have been closer to $200,000. Why would someone take such a loss like that? They might if they were afraid of ghosts!

Initially, Dave and Leslie thought there was only one ghost there. Soon it became apparent that their home and property were home to numerous wayward entities. Dave's initial feeling was that there was a male entity that didn't want him there and this seemed to be the case. He didn't. But then they recalled that Dave's grandson had seen the ghost of the "pretty woman with big boobies."

As time went on Dave started to notice things that were unusual around the house. He would see twinkles of light in the corner of a room or occasionally feel a cool breeze blow through when there was no source for it. He can always tell when an entity enters the area. Dave isn't afraid of ghosts and started to talk to the spirits that shared their house. When there would be evidence that one entered the room Dave would announce to them, "I know you're here, why don't you sit down and watch TV with us, that's cool." No problem.

That winter, one very cold evening Dave and Leslie lay in bed looking out the window at the trees outside. Suddenly, they saw some twinkling lights darting in and out from between the trees in the distance. The lights looked similar to fireflies but they weren't. The lights were constant except when they would go behind a tree. After a while, they noticed that the lights were moving closer to the house. As they neared the house the lights would gradually dim and then disappear altogether.

The brutal winter weather continued and this winter was very cold. It seemed to snow on a regular basis and the snowdrifts were getting deep. The Christensens had just recently moved in and they didn't have a tractor or any way to plow their long driveway. The only way to ensure that they'd be able to get to work the next morning was to park the car on a hill by the main road about an eighth of a mile away. To ensure the car would start the next morning, Dave would have to trek up there every night and start the car, letting it run and charge up the battery for a while. This was just a little added insurance. One evening as Dave headed out for the nightly car-starting ritual, he was forced to walk through the woods near the house because the snowdrifts were too deep out in the open. As Dave got closer to his car he heard children laughing, giggling and talking. Odd, he thought. It was nearly midnight, out in the middle of the country on a cold, raw night. The temperature outside was nearly thirty below and the wind was blowing like a banshee. What would kids be doing outside, here, at this hour? Dave was looking around wondering who was out there on this miserable night. He went ahead and started the car and let it run for about half an hour. While the car was warming up he went to check out the barn, thinking that maybe some neighbor kids were out playing around or playing jokes but this seemed pretty unlikely due to the weather and the late hour.

The next day when Dave made the trek to start the car he noticed something very strange. Footprints. Very small footprints. As he took the shortcut through the trees, he saw his footprints in the fresh snow. He also saw small children's footprints, like those of kids that were about four or five years old. The little footprints were up around the car and around the barn where Dave had just walked the night before. It kind of freaked him out. The little footprints came from the wooded area and followed Dave's movements from the night before and returned to the wooded area and abruptly stopped. It now became clear that there were children around. But on a cold windy night, how could Dave have possibly heard the children if they were off in the distance? In order to hear anything out in the open on a windy night like that you'd have to be pretty close but Dave hadn't seen any children. It began to sink in that his new home and land were home to numerous entities, many more than he had initially suspected.

Christmas soon arrived and the Christensens had company over like most families. Dave's grandson had just gotten a new remote-controlled car for Christmas. Of course, Santa had forgotten to get batteries for it so Dave went on a mission to the local convenience store in search of some double A and nine-volt batteries. When Dave returned from his battery mission, he was anxiously greeted and informed that the new remote-controlled car had taken off by itself, gone across the living room and then stopped. He initially thought that they were pulling his leg. "That's impossible, it can't do it by itself, it didn't have batteries," Dave stated. As Dave was explaining to everyone that there was no way this could happen the car suddenly took off again without warning. This time though, Dave was right there watching it and he hadn't put the batteries in it yet. It came across the room and hit Dave in the foot, as if to announce to him loud and clear that it was there. He got it. This particular entity appeared to be a child and liked to play.

One other night, Dave was in the living room watching TV when he saw something out of the corner of his eye that caught his attention. There was a little boy standing in their bedroom doorway peeking around the corner at Dave. When Dave spotted him, the little boy smiled at him and disappeared back into their bedroom. Startled, Dave went into the bedroom to investigate but didn't find anyone in the room.

On another occasion, Dave was outside on a cold winter night playing with the dogs, giving them some attention when he heard some whistling. It was some kind of tune. At first, he thought it was Leslie and he called her name but she didn't answer. Then he looked towards the road and saw a man walking towards him wearing a pair of jeans and a t-shirt. He had a dark complexion and appeared to be Hispanic. As he got closer to the house he simply vanished as Dave watched in amazement.

Another night, Dave was getting the dogs some water from the hose and when he looked up there was a woman standing by the corner of the new section of the house. Dave was surprised. The woman quickly turned and walked around the corner and out of sight. Dave went in the house, thinking it must have been Leslie and asked her if she had just been outside but she hadn't been. Dave was thinking that maybe someone was playing a joke on him and he again prodded Leslie about being outside but she insisted she had been inside. Dave thought, "Then who the hell was that?" He bolted back outside and around the back of the house. As he turned the corner he saw the woman again. She had a long dress down to her ankles and really long hair. She was now walking into the wooded area near their house. Dave jumped into his truck, turned on the headlights and drove around the wooded area to see if he could spot the woman again but she had disappeared.

Their house has a lot of activity and a lot of entities that live with them, not just the one or two that they had originally spotted. At night while they're in bed they can many times see shadows moving along their walls. They can also hear someone, or something, moving around the house and living room long after everyone has gone to bed. They continue to see the mysterious lights darting around in the trees at night. This happens year-round and they have ruled out bugs and insects. They had been in the house for about a year before they decided to take any photographs. They started by using their digital camera in order to save on developing costs and so they could plug the information directly into their computer. They immediately got some very interesting shots and know from the photos that there are numerous entities that live on their property. In some shots you can see as many as ten orbs. They were also able to get a picture of a spirit coming down from the trees that has a very ugly, nasty face. Dave went onto the computer and enhanced the color and played around with the different lighting to enhance the picture and it does appear to be a face in this particular picture.

Other clues point to supernatural entities. Animals are very keen to the supernatural and can sense them. The Christensens have six horses and for the longest time they would not go near the woods. They would walk all the way around the woods to get to the house when they could have taken a nice shortcut right through them. There is a nice place to cross through the woods and the grass is shorter but the horses refuse to take the shortcut, even when food is involved. On many occasions Dave would go into the pasture and pet and brush the horses and give them some attention. Then he'd go to the barn to get them some grain and he would take the shortcut through the woods. The horses, knowing the routine and that food was involved, would follow him right down to the tree line and stop. Then, when they would see Dave come out the other side of the trees, the horses would run around the woods, meeting Dave at the barn for some grain.

As summer arrived, Dave even tried moving the horse's water tank into the woods. He was thinking that the horses would like the shade and that the shade would help keep the water cleaner than if it was left in the open. The horses still refused to go into the wooded area and Dave was forced to move the tank back into the open.

Some friends of the Christensens offered to bring some dowsing rods over and see if they could find anything buried on their property out near the trees. In case you're not familiar with dowsing rods, they are metal rods that have a ninety-degree bend so you can hold them. What they will do is locate water, magnetic fields, graves and spirits/ghosts. You can fabricate some out of metal coat hangars if you want and these will work, guaranteed. When you locate one of the above things the rods will cross. In several locations the rods crossed, indicating there was some type of magnetic field change at that particular spot.

One spot in particular, the rods were confusing. When Kathy, a family friend, walked over this spot the rods would cross into each other. When she walked into that same spot from the other direction the rods would point outwards, away from each other. This was very unusual behavior, even for dowsing rods. They normally don't work in that manner, but they were. What was causing this strange reaction in the dowsing rods?

In that same general area, Dave decided to clean out some of the dead trees there and trim up the grass. Dave had his son, Richard, come out and help him. Dave hooked a chain around an old dead tree so he could pull it out and cut it up for firewood. Dave told Richard to go ahead and pull the tree out with the tractor and he started to. The old dead tree rolled over to one side, catching some of the dead branches on a live tree. The tractor came to a sudden stop and then, to Dave's horror, the chain tightened and the rear wheels walked out from under the tractor. What happened is that the tractor flipped over backwards with Richard on it. The odd thing about this is that as the tractor started to flip over, Richard came straight up off of the tractor seat, just like he was picked up and then dropped in just the right spot. When the tractor flipped over it narrowly missed Richard. By all accounts, the tractor should have flipped backwards right on top of Richard because that's where the seat is. Dave witnessed the event and is convinced that his son's life was saved by one of the many entities that reside on their property. How else can you explain a teenager defying gravity and flying straight up in the air? Was it just luck that the tractor missed him by mere inches? Why didn't he stay on the seat and ride it over backwards, as you would expect? Richard may have just made a new friend.

On numerous occasions, as Dave goes out at night to feed the dogs or horses that they keep, he will hear someone say, "Hi, Dave." Sometimes it's, "Goodnight." Other times, he will just hear voices or muffled talking. The closest neighbors are over half a mile away and it isn't them coming over to play pranks, it isn't the kids and all other options have been ruled out. So, who, or what is it?

Many times, doors will open or close by themselves in their house. The spirits can be helpful though. Several times, Dave would be looking for a tool or something around the house and simply could not find it. He has a technique that has now evolved to where if he can't find something, he simply asks his ghostly guests to help him out. If they find what he's looking for, he asks them to put it in plain sight so he can find it. That's worked several times. One time, Dave was at his wit's end looking for a special drill bit and had no luck finding it. He announced to his guests, "If any of you find the drill bit, please set it somewhere where I'll see it. The next day when he got up, the drill bit was sitting on the kitchen table. It wasn't there when he went to bed the night before and nobody else had put it there.

After Dave and Leslie decided to take some photographs in the house, they were surprised at what they saw. They took numerous photos with orbs in them. They also got shots of ectoplasm, which is a white, smoky looking entity. It is similar to cigarette smoke but is distinctly different and takes on more of a shape. A lot of the orbs are very large but they have a wide variety. They come in many different colors, kind of like the colored sparklers around the fourth of July. They come in white, green, red, blue and many variations of these. They range in size from a grape to the size of basketballs!

They now joke about their haunted house and have even come up with a nickname for it, The House on Haunted Hill. I think there's a movie with that title but this description fits their house to a T.

The events turned more ominous at their house recently. While in the process of working on this book project, tragedy struck. On the Sunday before Memorial Day, May 25, 2003, I had finished a draft copy of this book and e-mailed it to the Christensens. I then called them to let them know I had sent it but they were out so I left them a message on their answering machine. On Memorial Day I reached Leslie by phone and she was very excited about how the project was progressing. She was going to read the draft copy that day but they had to run some errands. I told her that I'd check back with her later in the week to see what she thought of the draft copy.

I tried to call the Christensens the following week and was surprised to find that their phone number was disconnected! Certainly if they were moving they would have mentioned that to me? The following weekend I finally reached Leslie on her cell phone and was shocked and saddened to learn that their house had burned down, the day after I e-mailed them the draft copy of the book! Coincidence?

The fire totaled the house and most of their possessions, including numerous one-of-a-kind photographs and videotapes of cases that they had worked on. Also destroyed were several photographs that we were going to include in this book. They had been downloaded onto a CD-ROM and were ready to mail to me but the fire got to it first. They had the originals on their computer but it was also destroyed and the hard drive could not be salvaged due to the extreme heat, which had literally melted the computer case. We did manage to salvage some pictures from their web site.

At first, they thought arson might be the cause. The day before the fire, on Sunday, Leslie was home and heard a knock at the door. She answered it and a teenager was there who used to live in the house, I'll call him Ray. Ray asked if Dave was home. Leslie explained that Dave was out running errands and wasn't home and Ray left, so Leslie thought. A few minutes later Leslie heard a few loud bangs. BANG, BANG! She rushed out the door and found Ray and a friend of his in their barn shooting rifles! They had opened the gates to the pastures and were trying to scare the six horses to get them to stampede. The plan backfired however, because the horses know who feeds them and instead of running off like the teenage delinquents had hoped for, the horses ran up to the house and stopped. Leslie was furious, and rightfully so. She yelled at the kids and told them to get off the property immediately. The next day, the house burned down. Odd.

The fire department immediately started looking into the fire to try and determine the cause. They pinpointed the location where the fire started, in a room that was currently used only for storage. The fire department determined that the fire started in the corner of the room, which happened to be Ray's old bedroom, on the wall about halfway up. Further investigation revealed that no traces of gasoline or any flammable liquids were used so this almost certainly ruled out arson. It was determined that the fire started on Memorial Day sometime prior to five o'clock in the afternoon, when the fire was first reported.

Ruling out arson, the fire department then tried to see if there was any other cause that could be found for this puzzling fire. In the wall where the fire started, there were no electrical cords or outlets near the ignition point and there were no candles or anything like that in the room that could explain the fire. At this point, everything was ruled out as a cause! The fire department could not pinpoint a cause and the official ruling is "undetermined." If there is

This is what was left of Dave and Leslie's house after the mysterious fire on May 26, 2003. No cause was found for the fire by the fire department. The final finding was "undetermined."

no logical explanation for the fire, how do you explain it? After all, something started the fire!

There are some very interesting things to note about the fire. The fire started in Ray's old bedroom, the kid who was at the door and shooting the rifle on their property. With arson ruled out, Ray was off the hook. The draft copy of this book was on a table within a few feet of where the fire started. Odd. Also, one of the three ghosts that Dave and Leslie have actually seen in human form in their house is the ghost of Ray's father. He was killed in a car accident about a year before they purchased the house. Is there a paranormal explanation for the fire? After all, there have been documented cases of poltergeist activity where there is spontaneous combustion and fires break out in homes, fires without any apparent cause. Could this explain what happened here? Did Leslie anger the ghost of Ray's father by kicking Ray off of their property the day before the fire? After all, the father still resides there! And how can a fire start on drywall with no ignition source? That just doesn't seem possible.

The Christensens have salvaged what belongings the fire didn't destroy and the house is going to be torn down and rebuilt. If there is a paranormal explanation for the fire, they are hoping that it calms down before their home is rebuilt.

This is a view from Ray's old room where the fire started. The fire started about three feet away from where the first draft of this book was located and no ignition source for the fire has ever been found.

Chapter 10

Jerry the Goat

This next case is from Council Bluffs, Iowa and involves a little deaf boy. It seems that the boy had "Jerry the Goat" bothering him. Jerry would steal the boy's toys and scare him. Occasionally the entity would hurt the boy. The mother became worried because the boy did not want to go play or sleep in his room anymore. If he had to go in there he would put all of his toys up on the window where Jerry could reach them. This way, the boy thought, Jerry could get his toys easily and would not hurt him. The boy told his mother that Jerry would hit and pinch him at night when he was in bed and this scared him.

Dave and Leslie received a call from the worried mother and made a trip over there to check out the house and interview the family.

On their second trip there, Dave and Leslie brought all of their equipment, including their video cameras and still cameras. They tried to get the boy to go to sleep in his own bed but he was scared to go in there by himself and so his mother finally went in there with him and laid down. After about an hour the boy finally fell asleep with the cameras rolling. Before the boy had fallen asleep, he was looking up at the ceiling and waving his hands saying, "Fly, Jerry, fly!" Dave and Leslie watched in amazement. About ten minutes after this the boy fell asleep and nothing unusual was seen on the monitors up to this point.

Suddenly, a very large orb floated down from the ceiling in the boy's room and came out the door and floated down the hallway. It was obvious that the boy was talking to something just prior to falling asleep, and something did appear to have been on the ceiling so logic would dictate that the boy was able to see something that had not originally been picked up on film.

During the course of this investigation, the Christensens made six trips to this house and discovered that there were actually three separate entities that resided with this family. At least one of these entities was Jerry, the one responsible for the hitting, pinching and harassment of the boy.

The three entities included one of a little girl, an adult male and an old woman. After doing their normal research, they discovered that a little girl had in fact died in a fire at the house back in the 1950's. There had been a family living there in the 1950's and the parents went out one night leaving an uncle to take care of the kids. The uncle fell asleep while smoking and the house caught on fire. Tragically, the fire killed a six-year-old girl.

On the fourth trip over to the house, they determined that the entity of the adult male was the uncle who started the fire. He was also the entity that was harassing the boy who lived there now.

The old woman was there but they were not sure what connection she had to the house.

The current owner's of the home wanted the entities out. Their boy was terrified and they wanted no part of hosting ghosts and allowing their family to be terrorized any longer; they were fed up with it. Dave has a way with talking entities out, nudging them to another place or getting them to cross over to where they should be. In this case, this was exactly what he was going to try and do.

Leslie filmed while Dave was attempting to talk the entities out of the house. Leslie was sitting in the boy's bedroom when it suddenly became very cold in there, a sure sign of paranormal activity. She had a sense that the entity of the little girl was there so she then sat on the bed and started to talk to her. This went on for about half an hour when Leslie felt something sit on her lap, yet nothing was there. Leslie could feel the weight of a child on her lap and she was chilled to the bone. Her lap was now especially cold and she knew that this was the presence of the little girl. Leslie began to rock her and talk to her. She was trying to convince her to go into the light and cross over and be with her family that had crossed over. This went on for nearly an hour.

Leslie then began to sense that something else was going on in the room. Instead of the intense cold, the room began to feel warm again. The air took on a tingling sensation and Leslie then felt the weight lift off her lap, although she did not see anything. Two other people were in the room at this time, the boy's mother and Brian who occasionally works with the Christensens. Brian is an outside observer from Creighton University in Omaha. As the weight lifted from Leslie's lap, Brian, who was standing in the doorway of the bedroom, suddenly broke out in tears. He couldn't explain it, he didn't know why he was crying. Leslie did. The little girl did cross over to be with her family and God. The atmosphere in the room had instantly changed and there was a very noticeable difference. Leslie herself was bawling like a baby. No words were necessary, everyone who was there knew what had just happened. That experience is one that Leslie will never forget. The feeling of warmth and love that happened when the spirit of the little girl crossed over is one that is almost indescribable, very moving. This is one of the things that keep Dave and Leslie going. Even though they occasionally encounter some truly frightening entities and situations, the ones like this where they really do some good and help out is what makes all the difference. The sense of accomplishment and being able to truly help someone in need keep the Paranormal Investigations team fired up and ready to take that next call.

Prior to the Christensens arriving to investigate this case, there were a number of unusual things that occurred in the house. The mother would find Camel cigarettes around various places in the house and she didn't know where they came from. Her boy was only six years old and he certainly wasn't smoking the Camels!

The spirit of the old woman was seen walking through the old patio on many occasions. The mother had a roommate for a while living with them who eventually moved out due to seeing the ghost of the old woman. She wanted no part of that.

After the spirit of the little girl left the house they believe that the spirit of the adult male also left. They did not deal with the spirit of the old woman and are not certain what has become of her. She's probably still there, although this entity never seemed to bother the family in any way and is welcomed to stay as long as she behaves.

After the investigation had concluded, things seemed to calm down in the house and the boy's mother was very happy with the outcome. Jerry the Goat had stopped bothering the boy and the house was relatively calm. All is now well.

Chapter 11

Fort Omaha

The Christensens received a phone call from a man who worked in the Maintenance Department at the college at Fort Omaha, also known as Metro Tech Community College, and he stated that there were unusual things going on at the college. One of the buildings was being renovated and the workers were complaining about things happening. They were very nervous and thought the place was haunted and many of the workers were afraid to work there. Some of the workers left and would not return. Tools had been dumped over for no apparent reason and some things had unexplainably been moved. Other things had happened too. He asked Dave and Leslie if they would be willing to come over and take a look at the building. They eagerly agreed and assembled the Paranormal Investigations team to start the investigative work.

Paranormal Investigations started the investigation by talking to people at the college. The Vice President of the college and his wife had previously lived in that building before the renovation started. The couple's daughter had a "friend" while living in the old building that was a ghost of a young girl. They interviewed two other people at the college who had actually seen an apparition in that same building. One of them saw a man walking to the building. The ghostly apparition was wearing an old cavalry uniform, was obviously a male and was walking towards the building that was now being renovated. The other witness had encountered a cavalry officer inside the old, historic building.

It seems that the building being renovated wasn't the only place at the college that hosted ghostly apparitions. Throughout the interviews of people on campus, scores of firsthand accounts of encounters with ghosts or ghostly apparitions emerged. There were several accounts of encounters in the main office area in the women's restroom, of all places. As women would proceed to the sink to wash their hands, they would look up into the mirror only to see the image of a cavalry officer standing there, staring back at them. There were several accounts from different witnesses who had seen the same apparition in this particular mirror. This building had previously been called Sherman Barracks in it's distant past. Originally it was a border fort for Omaha. The building was a barracks in the late 1800's and the apparitions that were seen here fit the description of the uniforms from that period of time long ago.

Other people described some of the odd things that occurred in building sixteen, the one that was currently being remodeled. In addition to hand and power tools being thrown around by unseen entities and power cords being tossed around, there was a serious problem of power tools that would turn themselves on, even when the cords had been unplugged! The workers were very concerned for their safety, as you can imagine. The workers were afraid to even go near the building. It got so bad that work on the remodeling project came to a grinding halt temporarily, as the workers refused to go into the building.

As they entered the building to investigate, Kel, one of the members of Paranormal Investigations, had a very strange vision of this building in its original condition. In the vision, he saw the original parlor room with a fireplace, piano and a sofa. On the sofa he saw a woman and a child. At the piano was another woman. At the fireplace was a man that was tall and slender with a mustache and hair down to his collar. He was wearing uniform pants and a bloused shirt, much like what they wore in the late 1800's. About two weeks after this incident the team was able to get a picture of this entity and the details match to a T the details of Kel's vision. Kel became somewhat nervous, as he had never seen a vision like this while working on any of the previous paranormal investigations.

The team from Paranormal Investigations was able to get some very interesting audio recordings of a voice of one of the entities. Leslie described the voice as sounding very demonic, although she did not feel that this entity itself was demonic.

One of the techniques that Dave likes to use in order to get an entity to show itself is to go into the location where it has been known to be active. He then will proceed to antagonize the entity by calling it chicken or demand that it show itself. Many times some activity will follow his taunting and they can get either video or photographs of the entity. Dave proceeded to use this technique here too. Normally, he tries to remain calm and not show any anger or fear towards the entity. However, in this case, he felt that the entity was playing games and acting like it was the spirit of a little girl, tricking them into believing it was something much different than what it really was. Dave went into the building with an attitude. Dave was angry and let the entity know that. He basically called the entity a jerk and may have injected a few other choice words. After this, the entity realized that the humans were able to hear it on the audio tape.

From this point on, whenever the team would leave their tape recorders on and leave a room they would return later only to find the tape recorders shut off. The only way they could get any recordings was to stay near the recorders to monitor them and ensure they were not tampered with. At the most, they would get about a minute of tape if they left the tape recorders alone from this point on. They also noticed that the entity would now stay one step ahead of them. They could tell that it would nearly always be one room ahead of them or occasionally it would sneak up behind them but it was always nearby, watching them. They tracked its movements using their various equipment, including their EMF meter.

After many weeks of investigation they struck gold and got this one shot of what they believe is Captain Jack peering out the window. They could not find any source for a reflection and believe this picture is the real deal.

The building under renovation was very spooky in the dark and also very dangerous. It was a three-story building and the railings from the stairways had been removed for the renovation. One wrong step and it could spell disaster.

On one evening during the investigation, Leslie and her friend Darby left the building for a breather and to review their tapes when Darby noticed that she had black smears or streaks on her legs. It looked like someone, or something, had grabbed her legs. When she went to wipe off the substance she found that her legs were bruised, although she had no recollection of being touched while in the old building. It was apparent that the substance and bruises had just recently gotten on her legs but she didn't feel it happen. How is that possible?

The investigation lasted about six weeks and on about the fourth week, the team was growing somewhat alarmed. One of the entities there was very powerful. It seemed to be keeping a very close eye on the team as they came there week after week. It was closely following them from room to room and would frequently double back on them. They could tell this by using their equipment, which for this case included electromagnetic field meters (EMF Meters), an oscilloscope, video equipment with nightshot, three cameras and audio recording equipment. The EMF meters are a quick easy way to tell if there is an entity nearby and the meter readings clearly showed that whatever they were following would frequently turn up following them! To find the entity, they would simply follow the readings on the oscilloscope.

Notice the misty-looking form in this picture taken outside the eerie building that was being renovated. This is just one form a ghost can take. This is not a reflection and no cause could be found for the abnormal shape in this photo.

They would normally set their equipment up on the third floor near the open stairwell. They were trying to determine which direction the strongest meter readings were coming from. Dave would move the sensor to where they would get the highest reading. The strongest readings were coming from a bedroom at the back of the stairs in the southeast corner of the building. Dave carefully moved the sensor into the suspect room and the oscilloscope readings were definitely higher, by about three clicks on the screen. After a few minutes, they would move the sensor about three feet further into the room and they would let it sit for a few more minutes and they would take another reading. With each progression farther into the room, the oscilloscope readings would get higher, indicating that the energy was stronger. They felt very strongly that the entity was hiding or used this room most often but now they wanted to pin him, or it, down and find its exact hiding place. Dave progressively moved the sensor now towards the closet in the room and Kel moved into the room and began taking pictures, hoping to get the entity on film. The closet door was off for the renovation and they had a clear view of the inside of the closet.

Dave now moved the sensor directly in front of the closet and the oscilloscope readings jumped about four times higher than they were before the last move. Kel moved into the closet to take some pictures. When the first flash went off in the closet, a very loud, guttural groan rang out from there, startling the team. It sent a chill down their spines. There was a swishing sound and very unexpectedly, Dave lifted off the floor about three feet and was thrown into the wall about eight feet away, back first. He slowly slid down the wall and sat there for a moment, collecting his thoughts. Then he got up and dusted himself off. He wasn't injured but he was definitely shaken up. The team very cautiously approached the closet and listened. They could hear mortar from between the bricks hitting the floor below. Kel ran over to an opening in the floor and looked down with a flashlight. He could actually see the mortar falling from the closet wall and land on the floor below. The entity had retreated through the back of the closet and gone to the floor below to escape the nosy intruders.

The team had to take a break after this stunning series of events so they could collect their thoughts. Before leaving the room they took a few more pictures. Dave needed a break and a cigarette after being thrown across the room by the unseen entity so he decided to go outside for a few minutes for some fresh air. Leslie and Darby also went down the stairs to the first floor and went outside with Dave. Kel had gone over to the closet to check out the opening that the entity went through and to examine the mortar that had been knocked out. After a few moments outside, Darby realized that Kel wasn't outside with them and he must have been still in the building somewhere. It was now well after dark and the building had no power due to the renovation in progress. The only source of light was from the flashlights that the team had brought along. Kel must have been left alone in the dark, Darby thought. Leslie and Darby carefully made their way up the stairs with no railing, back up to the third floor. They found Kel in the same spot, squatting by the closet in the dark. They asked him what he was doing and he replied, "Just sitting here." Darby then asked why he didn't come downstairs and Kel replied, "Because it's dark and I didn't want to go down there alone." It didn't take them long to understand what he was talking about. They had just witnessed the awesome power of this unseen entity. They had just seen their friend picked up and hurled eight feet across the room by something that they couldn't see! If it could pick up Dave and throw him across the room, what's stopping this entity from throwing one of them down one of the open stairwells? Kel was concerned about simply falling down one of the stairwells because he didn't have a flashlight with him and it was pitch dark in the old building at night with no electricity on. None of them wanted to take any chances now and the three of them wisely decided to take a break outside. They made their way safely down the stairs and out of the building.

After about an hour, the team returned inside the building for a few more hours of tense investigation.

After safely returning home they started to pour over their findings. They did get the bone-chilling groaning on tape along with some voices of the entities. They were initially disappointed because they found nothing unusual on the pictures that they had developed of the room on the third floor that Dave was thrown across. They were certain that they would see something on those shots! Nothing appeared to be out of the normal, even in the sequence of shots where Dave was hurled across the room. However, after about the fourth time reviewing the pictures, Darby noticed something very unusual. In the shots of the closet you could clearly see an even-colored floor. This was due to the thick layer of dust from the remodeling and you could clearly see the floor had not been walked on in the closet. In a picture taken of the closet after Dave was thrown across the room, Darby noticed footprints in the closet. The unusual thing was that the footprints were coming out of the closet, not in! These were not Kel's footprints, they were taken before he had gone to the closet.

Dave and Leslie also found that they had gotten a picture of the male entity wearing the cavalry uniform that they later nicknamed Captain Jack.

The college desired to keep the story quiet but a faculty member had called the Omaha World Herald and filled them in about the strange occurrences that were going on at the college. The faculty member had a friend that was a writer for the paper and he wrote an article about the strange events. After the story hit the media the college wanted the investigation to immediately stop; they didn't want any more publicity related to the ghostly events.

Dave felt that there were several entities at the college. Kel's vision helped convince the team that there were at least three entities at the college. There was Captain Jack, two women and the girl that lived in the building being renovated. He was convinced that while they investigated the building being renovated (building sixteen), Captain Jack was playing cat and mouse with them pretty much the entire time.

Paranormal activity has been reported in several of the other buildings on campus. Dave and Leslie were given a tour of the campus and took EMF meter readings in a number of the buildings. They noted especially high EMF meter readings in the building that once housed the military hospital. In the basement of the old military hospital they noted very high readings and later found that this area was once the morgue many years ago. There have been reports of entities in the form of Indians, women, children and then old Captain Jack himself in several areas of the campus.

In the Maintenance building where the college stores their vehicles, the building has a very high ceiling. It has been reported that people have seen the shadows of figures hanging from the ceiling of this building. Further investigation revealed that the building was once used to execute prisoners by hanging.

There was an incident in the late 1800's when an Indian named Standing Bear was arrested and taken to Fort Omaha for trial. Many of the Sioux Indians gathered there and camped out on the parade grounds so they could be there for the trial. Could this possibly have anything to do with the ghostly Indian apparitions that have been reported there?

Another interesting footnote to this case is that Paranormal Investigations had two faculty members along on the case and they brought their own audio tape recorders and cameras with them. The faculty members had also found some very unusual voices and sounds on their audio tapes. In addition to that, they also found some strange images on their pictures. Initially, the faculty members were very skeptical of the whole idea of the ghost hunt but after actually being there and having those bodily sensations, they are now firm believers. The old saying that a picture is worth a thousand words holds very true, especially when you are dealing with a subject like the paranormal. This helped to lend some credibility to Paranormal Investigations as far as the college was concerned. There are some quacks out there in the paranormal investigation field and a few bad eggs can give all of them a bad rap. For this very reason, Dave, Leslie and their team always go out of their way to ensure the integrity of their investigations. For example, they always have a witness present, not only for insurance reasons, but more importantly to see the paranormal activity first hand, in person. The witness could be a police officer, professor from a local college, homeowner, TV reporter or friend of the family. It doesn't really matter as long as someone else is there to stand up and say, "Hey, I was there and saw what happened. These guys are for real. I got the same thing on film that they did."

For about a year after the investigation, the Christensens received e-mails from some of the faculty members at the college asking them to continue with the investigation but the college wanted no part of it now. They absolutely did not want any more publicity and did not want the college to be known for paranormal activity. Building sixteen has been turned into offices and there was still plenty of paranormal activity going on there after the investigation had concluded. It's likely going on to this day.

Chapter 12

Mormon Cemetery

Mormon Cemetery is located in North Omaha and is a historic site where the Mormons would set up winter camps. The original name of the camp at the time was The Winter Encampment, back in the 1800's. At this location the Mormons suffered one of their worst winters ever while camping in Nebraska and hundreds of them perished due to the severe cold and harsh conditions.

The Christensens received a few phone calls from a woman we'll call Mrs. Smith (name has been changed to protect her identity). Mrs. Smith recalled to the Christensens that one evening her husband, son and she heard a woman crying up in the cemetery. Mrs. Smith sent her husband and son up to the cemetery to see if the woman was OK or if she needed any help. They went into the cemetery but did not find the woman but could hear her crying. As they neared the area where the crying was coming from it abruptly stopped. The duo wandered around for about twenty minutes, looking for the distraught woman but found no sign of her and returned home.

A few days later, they again were outside enjoying the nice evening and they again heard the woman crying. This time, however, the crying seemed much louder. Mrs. Smith again insisted that her husband and son find this woman and see if they could find her and help her or at least find out why she was crying. While they were in the cemetery they could still hear the crying but they were having a hard time trying to find where the woman was. They described the crying sound as coming from all around them, not just one specific place. This puzzled them and they again were not able to locate the mystery woman who was so distraught. They again left the cemetery without finding any sign of the woman.

Mrs. Smith soon called the Christensens back with this new information. Dave was initially skeptical and was looking at the other cases they had to work on so they put this one off temporarily.

They finally got a chance to go meet with Mrs. Smith in the late fall of that year. Dave, Leslie and another couple who work with them made their way into the cemetery on a chilly fall evening. They brought with them video cameras, still cameras and electromagnetic field meters (EMF meters) and set up their equipment in different areas of the cemetery. They were hoping to capture the woman crying on either videotape or audio tape. They were not disappointed. About 11:30 p.m. they heard the sound of a woman whimpering, although it was not very loud. The sound was coming from all around them, just like what Mr. Smith and his son had described to them. In order to try and pinpoint the origin of the sound they began to walk around the cemetery, leaving their video equipment in place to silently monitor part of the old cemetery. They took several photographs of the area and they observed that the EMF meter readings were quite high. They were very confident that some type of activity was taking place right then. The EMF-meter readings right then were 38.4 which is very high. A normal house, for example, will have EMF meter readings anywhere between 0.0 and maybe 2, if there are some appliances on. 38.4 is extremely high, especially when there is no known source for the high readings. Some things that might cause a high reading like that would be if you are within inches of a TV screen, refrigerator or some type of appliance that has some electronics in it. High voltage power lines can cause high EMF meter readings like that but they did not find this to be the case. They were in the middle of an old Mormon cemetery with no power lines anywhere to be seen. There was no source that they could see that would cause the unusually high meter readings. This being said, they were convinced that paranormal activity was present around them.

The whimpering soon stopped and as it stopped, the EMF meter readings dropped down to the normal range that one would expect for this area. Whatever it was seemed to have left the area, for now at least.

The next day they took their film over to the local one-hour photo shop at K-Mart. When they claimed their film and looked over the pictures they were excited to see some unusual images. They found shots that included not only the headstones and trees, but also ectoplasm in the shape of faces. Ectoplasm on film looks similar to cigarette smoke, but they were not smoking while they worked. Also, ectoplasm is shaped differently than cigarette smoke. If you really study a photograph of ectoplasm and put it side-by-side with a faked photograph of cigarette smoke or even your breath on a chilly night, you can clearly see the difference. Ectoplasm will take on different shapes and many times if you look closely at the center mass you will see an orb.

In one shot, they found ectoplasm to the left of the camera and there was also an unusual image above them. They enlarged the photograph on their computer and were surprised to see the image of a woman who appeared to be floating well above them. Her long hair was blowing behind her and she was cradling something in her hands. When they zoomed in the photo even more they could see that what she was cradling was a baby.

The Paranormal Investigations team returned to the cemetery to see if they could find the entity of this woman with her child but they were unsuccessful. They found other entities in the area to be sure, but they did not come across the woman and the child again. They concluded that there certainly were, and are, entities in this cemetery. Mrs. Smith can rest assured that she is not crazy, the woman sobbing was real, although not alive. Why she was crying will remain a mystery for now. Maybe she was saddened by the death of her child or family members on that harsh Nebraska winter that claimed so many lives. We may never know, but we do know that the spirits are indeed restless in the old Mormon Cemetery.

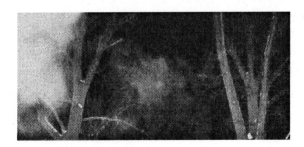

This picture shows the eerie mist to the left and the mist between the two trees. Dave and Leslie believe the mist between the trees may be the mysterious woman crying.

Chapter 13

Elkhorn Cemetery

The Elkhorn Cemetery is an old German cemetery located in Elkhorn, Nebraska. Paranormal Investigations heard reports that people had seen ghostly figures wandering around amongst the headstones at night. They received several more calls about this particular cemetery and finally decided to investigate these claims. They decided to survey the layout of the cemetery during the daylight hours prior to starting the evening investigation so they would know where any potential hazards were located. There was a road that ran all around the cemetery and through the back of the old Potters field. The Potters field was located in the back of the cemetery and there was a thick tree line and overgrown bushes in the back area of the cemetery, creating a very spooky atmosphere at night.

The first evening that they ventured into the cemetery, they had a pretty good idea of what the back area looked like. Dave and Leslie had purchased new batteries for their flashlights and equipment. They were eager to start the investigation.

They took the road into the back part of the cemetery, parking about halfway back. From there they walked. The electromagnetic field meter (EMF meter) was very normal but Leslie did pick up some fluctuations and began to follow them from near the back of the cemetery to the main highway. Dave was about thirty feet behind her. Suddenly, the EMF meter spiked up to fifteen, which is pretty high, especially with no power source nearby. Leslie yelled at Dave to quickly take a picture. But, before he could get a single picture taken he found Leslie standing right next to him. Leslie doesn't scare easily but something had just set her off. Dave chuckled about this, mentioning that she was supposed to be up there investigating, not standing here right next to him. Leslie stayed just a little closer to her husband than normal as they continued to investigate this eerie cemetery.

Dave took several pictures as they walked along the dark, still cemetery. Several minutes later, they started to make their way to the back of the cemetery. Leslie continued to watch her EMF meter when Dave suddenly and firmly said to her, "Walk back to the truck. Don't turn around, just walk back to the truck." She asked him why but he replied, "Just go as quickly as you can get back to the truck and I'll be right behind you!" Leslie didn't need any further prodding and she quickly made her way back to the truck. Leslie suddenly noticed she didn't hear Dave's footsteps behind her and this caused her some alarm. On this particular night he was wearing his cowboy boots with spurs on them and she could easily hear where he was. Now, she heard nothing but silence. She turned around to see Dave standing in the cemetery road. He took a few pictures and when the flash went off Leslie could see a man standing there, close to Dave. He was dressed like a farmer, with a plaid shirt on. He was just standing there with his arms crossed, staring at them. Dave turned around and told Leslie to get going and get into the truck. They wasted no time and quickly jumped into the truck and quickly left the old dark cemetery.

After making the ritual trek to the one-hour photo shop at the local K-Mart, they received the film back and were very surprised to find the entire roll of film blank! Instead of finding the picture of the man standing there with his arms crossed they were looking at blank film. They have never had that happen before and they were not sure if there was some type of problem with the camera or some other event that caused the film to come out blank. They decided to make another trip there and assembled the Paranormal Investigations team. They arrived after dark and started to once again look for any signs of paranormal or unusual activity. This time there were four of them instead of just Dave and Leslie. Leslie and Darby started at the front of the cemetery and began to walk towards the back taking meter readings with the EMF meters. On this night, they noticed a very unusual smell. When they neared a particular entity it smelled like fire, a house fire, as Leslie described it. They continued to follow the unusually high EMF meter readings and as they got closer to the entity the fire smell grew stronger. As they closed in, they were able to actually see a gray-colored orb moving back and forth between the various headstones. The men were fairly close behind them at this point.

The women continued to follow the entity and the strong fire smell and it led them away from the men. They soon found themselves at the highest point of the cemetery, and also the darkest. The men were now down at the base of the cemetery and they didn't know where the women had gone. Leslie and Darby wisely decided to retreat for now and made their way back down the hill and met up with Kel and Dave at the base of the hill. Leslie and Darby explained to the men the sensation of the strange fire smell and told about the unusually high meter readings. They now noticed that as they moved away from the entity it now seemed to be following them! The meter readings were fluctuating somewhat but were mostly constant. This would indicate that the entity that they had found was keeping a set distance from them but was certainly nearby and this made Leslie and Darby a little nervous. They told the men to stay behind them and to not wander off too far. This seemed to be an opportune time and the men decided to play a little joke on the women. Dave took off his boots and sneaked up behind Leslie, gently putting his hand on her shoulder. Needless to say, she freaked out. Leslie thought at that very moment, "It's got me, this is it, it's all over!" She fell to the ground yelling and screaming, kicking her feet in the dark cemetery. Dave was pretty amused by this and got a good laugh out of it. Darby had seen Dave sneaking up on Leslie but was still scared herself and was jumping up and down, screaming along with Leslie. The tension had seemed to get the best of them. Leslie realized at that moment that if an entity ever did try to get her that it would be all over. She'd just collapse in a heap and die because the fright would cause her to get Gumby legs and she would be able to do nothing but lie there and scream. Dave was pretty sure he was in trouble that evening but lucky for him, Leslie has a good sense of humor and they laughed about it all the way home. Leslie was embarrassed by the way she reacted that evening. Dave decided that it was in his best interest if he didn't pull that stunt again, at least for a while!

They made another trip there and purchased new batteries for the flashlights and equipment. On the first evening trip to the cemetery, the flashlights all went dead after only about thirty to forty-five minutes of use. This was very unusual that they would all go dead that quickly, especially because they had just purchased new batteries before that trip there. The odd thing about the first trip there was that Leslie had put one of the dead flashlights on the dashboard of the truck as they jumped in to leave in a hurry. As they exited the cemetery and turned onto Maple, the main road, the flashlight suddenly came on and worked fine after leaving there. Odd.

They made sure they had brand-new batteries for this venture to the cemetery. Once again, within half an hour, the batteries were all dead in the flashlights, all of them. Whatever was there did not want them to see it. The second evening trip there they were able to get some very good photographs. This time they did not have any problems with the film coming out blank. Several of the photographs included pictures of orbs. One of the orbs was huge and looked like a large ball of fire. This made sense to them now. They believed the smell was coming from one of the many entities that roamed the dark cemetery.

In one photo two orbs are visible going into the trees. They had a series of photos of the orbs and you can see how they were moving by looking at their progression in the photos. They did not have any luck recording voices at the cemetery and had not taken their video equipment for this investigation. They had only the photographs and their recollection of the events that they witnessed.

When Leslie and Darby were in the cemetery they were very afraid. They noticed that as they got farther away from the men their EMF meter readings increased greatly, as did the fire smell. As they got closer to Dave and Kel, the EMF meter readings dropped significantly and the fire smell grew more faint. They believe that the entity, for whatever reason, was trying to separate the men and the women. As the women came closer to the men the entity would back off but keep a constant distance. When the men would move even thirty to forty feet away, the entity would move in fairly close. They knew it was nearby, watching them. They were the ones being hunted, not the ghosts. The women sensed this and their fear was growing.

At one point Leslie and Darby sat down and let the entity that reeked like fire get close, almost too close! As the entity approached them, Darby was struck with a vision of an old farmhouse in flames with two children in it. In her vision she saw the man in the plaid shirt enter the house as it burned. He was apparently attempting to get the children out. There was no wife or woman in the vision, only the children and man in the plaid shirt. The entity was right there with them at this point, and the fire smell was overpowering. Leslie actually felt the entity touch her and could smell the fire smell very strongly. She knew it was right there with them. After about four to five minutes Leslie developed a strong pain in her stomach but she wasn't sure why. The incident left both Leslie and Darby very shaken and to date, they have been too frightened to return to this particular cemetery. They were very aware of the intense fear that gripped them and they sensed danger there. This cemetery is not a place to take lightly or to mess around with. The dead should be respected and left alone here, unless you have nerves of steel.

The entity with the plaid shirt was seen wandering around the cemetery on a few occasions as they neared the driveway. They could see a gray form wandering between the headstones and trees but when they would get just a little closer, it would vanish.

Leslie and Darby got the distinct impression that they were not wanted or welcomed at the Elkhorn Cemetery. They decided to trust their instincts and to date, they have not returned. *Some things are best left alone.*

Printed in the United States
36957LVS00007B/240